ENCOURAGEMENT FROM HEAVEN

Words of Strength from On High

Dr Ekaete Ukpong

Global Synapses

ENCOURAGEMENT FROM HEAVEN
ISBN: 978-978-988-586-2
Volume 2

Published by:
GLOBAL SYNAPSES NIG. LTD.

First Edition

For permissions, inquiries, or bulk purchase requests, please contact:

GLOBAL SYNAPSES NIG. LTD.
56 Army Jetty Road,
Ekorinim 2, Cross River State
Phone: +2348036716154
Email: synapsesglobal@gmail.com

Connect with Dr. Ekaete V. Ukpong:
Facebook: Dr Ekaete Ukpong
Instagram: @dr_ekaeteukpong
X (Twitter): @DrEkaeteUkpong

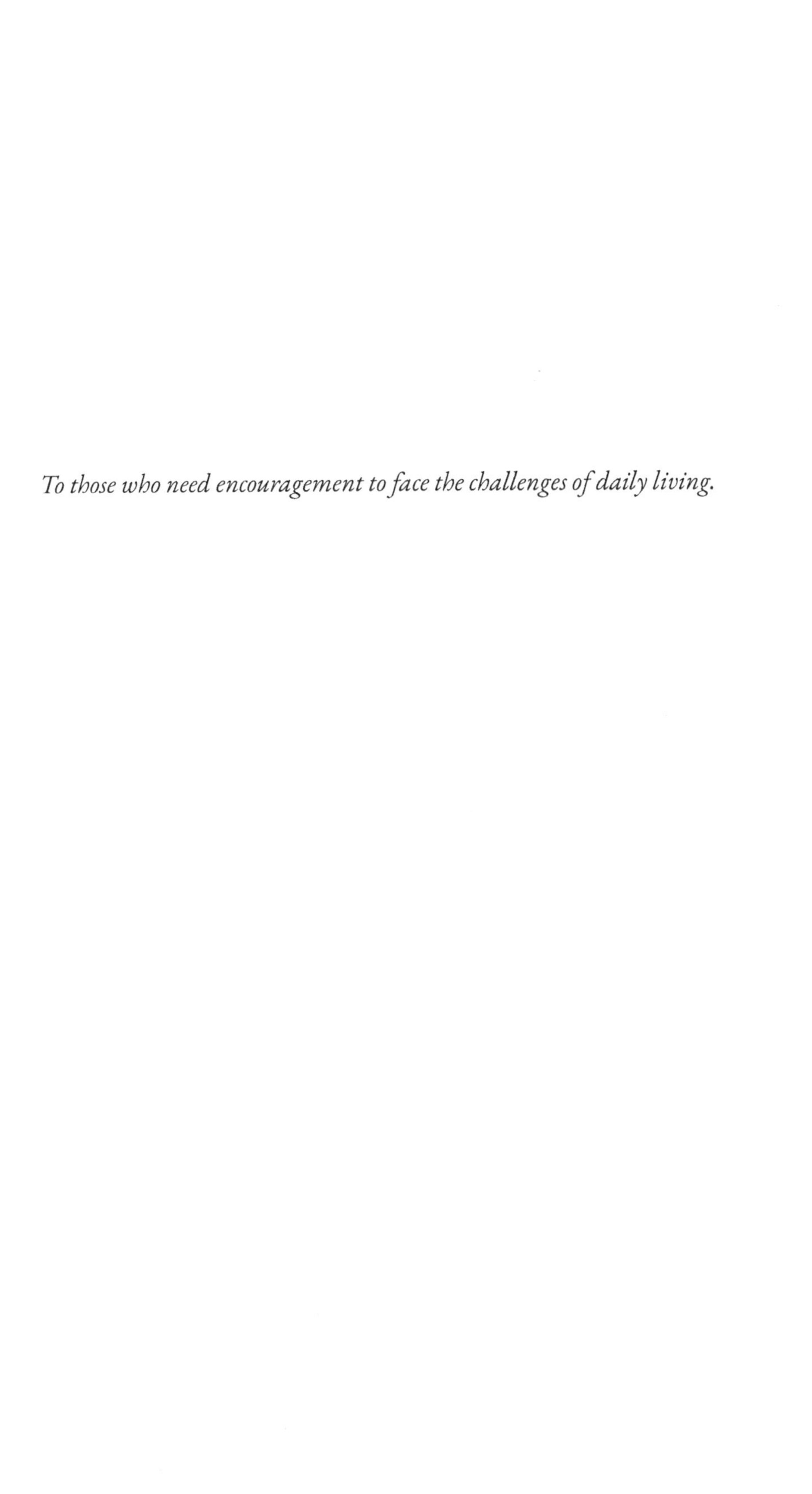

To those who need encouragement to face the challenges of daily living.

Foreword

No one fails to recognise a good meal! Some may judge the dish by the aroma, others by its look or appearance, but the age-old adage "that the taste of the pudding is in the eating" stands true. Here, you have an invitation to three months of feasting in the WORD of LIFE! There is no better invitation than this. Especially when it offers ENCOURAGEMENT FROM HEAVEN, to a world made of wounded pilgrims.

This book is a three-month invitation to a richly prepared banquet designed to add spiritual "flesh and sinews" to every passionately hungry believer. From the assurance that Carpenters are sent on assignment for the believer through faith requirements for asking and receiving (you will learn to ask rightly), the need for patience, all open the reader up to great expectations. There is the all-time godly counsel to take time to look into one's past to repay and rebuild the waste places. This is the panacea for receiving divine acceleration.

The reader is guided through what to do in times of waiting. Fear, a common enemy of faith and godliness must be conquered. There is a call to 'speak not their language' especially because God hears, watches our thoughts and will always respond to us, with answers particularly for specific requests. Some of these challenges require one to move out of the comfort zone, to watch and pray and fight against depression and other unpleasant circumstances. The presentation of each meal gives no room for indigestion and constipation. Every seeking reader will find each day, a rich and balanced diet.

A word of caution though! Do not read this daily manual if you do not intend to change in some area of your life. Of course, you will find it interesting, exciting and instructive. Good as these are, they are far from the reason for this devotional guide. This one is intended to produce change! The kind of change that will see believers living out the realities of the word of God drawn from studies outlined here that lead the reader to an intimate experience and encounter with God's word! And I think this is heaven's intention for releasing the revelations presented in this beautiful material.

Saying it will bless you will be saying the obvious. I recommend it to all and sundry as a must have, must read, necessary companion for a quarter of the year. You will be glad you used it!

Happy reading.

Right Rev. Prof. Nneoyi Egbe
Bishop, Archdioceses (Anglican Communion)
Calabar

How To Use This Book

1. Thank God, to open the heavens for your understanding.
2. Pray for revelation of the word.
3. Read every Bible scripture for each day.
4. Follow and obey every instruction specified each day.
5. Personalize every prophetic declaration of each day.
6. Believe and receive the word into your spirit.
7. Use the prayer guideline for each day.
8. Rejoice in the word always while thanking God for answers given.

God bless you!

Introduction

Many today are discouraged, downcast, heart-broken, depressed, and hopeless due to the prevailing challenges and the peculiar battles they fight in their daily living. However, there is a solution to these negativities for those who are interested.

God never leaves his children comfortless; he makes a way of escape for every challenge facing those who trust in him. Challenges do not necessarily mean life is over. They sometimes mark a bend or a pause. Challenging times can sometimes be a purifying furnace to bring out the best in a man. Man was not created to face challenges in life, but sin brought hardships, struggles, poverty, lack, sickness, deprivation, degradation, and battles to man. These, the devil uses as avenues to cause discouragement and gain victories over the ignorant.

The strength one needs to face life's challenges cannot come from a broken, depressed, hopeless state of man. Every man needs encouragement to rise from the dust and face challenges. David encouraged himself, backed by the word of God, as he returned home from battle to see that his family and his people had been led away captives. He received strength to pursue and recover all that was taken from him.

> ***And David was greatly distressed; for the people spake of stoning him, because the soul of all the people was grieved, every man for his sons and for his daughters: but David encouraged himself in the LORD his God* (1 Samuel 30:6).**

Encouragement from heaven gives strength, brings back lost hope, restores joy to the downcast and depressed, boosts our faith to face challenges, gain victory over the devil and fulfill our glorious destiny. These daily words will bring good news to the poor, heal the broken hearted, and open prison doors to those that are in captivity.

My prayer for you is that the Holy Spirit will gain you access to the mysteries and spirit behind every word sent and encourage you to fight and win all your battles. As you daily meditate on these words of encouragement from heaven, may your strength be greatly renewed; you shall mount up with wings as an eagle; you shall run and not be weary; you shall walk and not faint.

Be encouraged from heaven!

Day 1

The Coming of the Carpenters

Bible Reading: Zachariah 1:16-21

"Then said I, What come these to do? And he spake, saying, These are the horns which have scattered Judah, so that no man did lift up his head: but these are come to fray them, to cast out the horns of the Gentiles, which lifted up their horn over the land of Judah to scatter it." (Zachariah 1:21).

Good morning, Children of the Merciful God, His loving kindness and faithfulness endure forever, hallelujah!

Brethren, God can do exceedingly abundantly above what we can imagine. Whatever the enemy built can be pulled down, whatever the enemy planted can be uprooted, whatever the enemy scattered can be gathered, and whatever has a beginning also has an end. God's mercy endures through all generations.

The children of Israel sinned against God, their fathers disobeyed the commandment of the Lord, and God allowed the horns of the Gentiles to scatter them, lead them into captivity, put them in bondage, and none could lift his head. What did these horns do? They scattered Judah, Israel, and Jerusalem. Judah represents praise in your life, Israel represents your prevailing with God, and Jerusalem represents your peace.

Have the horns scattered praise out of your life that you can no longer praise God? Have troubles, sorrow, agony, tears, murmuring, and complaints taken over your soul? When last did you give God heartfelt praise? A horn has scattered your Israel. The horn scattered your Judah that you no longer praise God as afore time. How is your prayer life? Are you prevailing in the place of prayer? Are you struggling and praying with no result or answers to your prayers?

Has peace been taken away from your soul, home, environment, marriage, church, family, job, and all areas of life **(2 Chronicles 15:5)**? The horn has scattered your Jerusalem. Some horns resulted from what your fathers did. Generational curses in families are working against their progress. However, today God says, He has had mercy upon you. God has released the four carpenters to fray and cast out these horns. God has cast out the horns that took away your praise, the answers to your prayers, and peace. You will look for the horns and not find them forever.

The word of the Lord is sent to someone today, saying, "I am jealous for Jerusalem and for Zion with a great jealousy" **(Zechariah 1:14)**. He says, "I have seen the cry of my people, and I have come down to deliver them out of the hand of their taskmasters" **(Exodus 3:7)**. God has released his carpenters into your homes, ministry, family, marriage, job, environment, business, world, and entire life; to fray and cast out every horn that had taken away your peace, praise, joy, and victorious prayer life.

Someone is about to break forth into singing, someone's home is about to experience a breakthrough, and someone's story is about to turn around. Rejoice, again I say rejoice, the Lion of the tribe of Judah has prevailed, He has cast out the horns of the Gentiles. Jerusalem shall yet be built up.

PRAYER: *Father, thank you for your word. As you said it, so do it unto us. I pray that we shall not shut our doors to these restoration angels. Please help us to receive the carpenters sent to deliver us. Let these ancestral horns lose our addresses. Restore peace, joy, praise, and strength in the place of prayer and our connectivity with you; we wait on you, Oh Lord. Thank you, Father, for answers, in Jesus' name.*

Day 2

You Need Faith!

Bible Reading: Romans 10:12-17

***"So then, faith cometh by hearing and hearing by the word of God"* (Romans 10:17).**

Good morning, Family of the Living God, He is faithful, hallelujah!

Brethren, faith is what you need to please God and have all your needs met. A man of faith is a man that knows no impossibility because faith raises you to the class of God **(Matthew 19:26, Mark 9:23)**.

Faith is a universal currency that can purchase anything from the heavenly realm. You cannot please God without faith, but you can move any mountain with it. David triumphed by faith. Moses led the children of Israel out of the bondage of 430 years by faith. Gideon triumphed by faith. Abraham became blessed in all things by faith. Hannah gave birth to a great Prophet (Samuel) by faith. Mary conceived and brought forth Jesus by faith. Sarah received the strength to deliver Isaac at 90 years old by faith.

Paul came as the least of the Apostles and wrote two-thirds of the New Testament by faith **(Hebrews 11)**. The list goes on and on.

The book of Acts of the Apostle is not closed with Amen; hence, your name can be added **(Acts 28:31)**. How did these great men and women receive the faith to wrought these great works? Faith was activated in them by encounters with the word of God. Something was fired up inside of them when He spoke to them. Their confidence built up; they knew nothing could stop them. They moved up to the realm of possibilities and came out with mighty works. Faith only comes as you keep hearing and hearing the word of God **(Romans 10:17)**. We keep struggling with a particular challenge because we have not heard enough to feed our faith in that area of our life.

Do you want your healing? Then go for the word of healing. Do you need deliverance? Go for the word of deliverance. Is it marriage? Seek for the word concerning marriage. You do not keep hearing the word on financial prosperity when you need healing and expect to receive your healing. The day your faith is built up concerning your challenge is the day of your deliverance from it.

Do you want positive things to happen to you and keep hearing the negatives? Then you are far from your expectations. You need faith to move that mountain; you must keep hearing and hearing what God's word is saying concerning it. David never stopped hearing each time he needed victory; he went for the word concerning that challenge. Moses never stopped hearing and hearing from God, and in the end, he conquered Pharaoh and the whole of Egypt.

The faith of yesterday is not sufficient for today. The day you stop hearing from the Lord is when your faith begins to dwindle and finally fails. Faith fails if you do not constantly feed it with the word. There is no impossibility with God. With faith, all things are possible **(Mark 9:23)**. Rise then, go for the word of faith, go again and again.

The good news is that someone's word is sent for his deliverance now. The word shall build your faith to overcome that challenge facing you.

Hear, believe, receive, and overcome!

PRAYER: *Father, thank you for your word. Teach us how to build up our faith, help those who sit at ease in Zion, and help us hear your word and see it. Increase our faith to surmount this mountain before us. Give us a testimony of a lifetime. Thank you, Father, for answers, in Jesus' name.*

Day 3

Ask and Receive!

Bible Reading: 1 Kings 3:5-13

"In Gibeon the Lord appeared to Solomon in a dream by night: and God said, Ask what I shall give thee" **(1 Kings 3:5).**

Good morning, Family of The Prayer-Answering God. He is too faithful to fail.

Brethren, God does not have a store house for unanswered prayers. God is a prayer-answering God and He is a promise-keeping God. As He says it, He is committed to making it come to pass. However, not everyone understands the principles of asking and receiving their desired answers from God.

All through the scriptures, selfish, self - centred prayers never met God's approval **(James 4:3, 1 Kings 19:4, Luke 22:42, Jonah 4:2-3).** Some do not ask at all but expect God to give to them and they do not receive because they have not asked **(John 16:24).**

Some ask not according to God's will for their lives but according to their ambition and the lust in their heart; the answers also do not come **(1 John 5:15)**. Some do not ask in faith in the name of Jesus **(Mark 11:24, John 14:14)**. Some ask without optimistic anticipation **(James 1:6-8)** and the answers are farfetched. How then are we to ask to please the Lord?

The Solomon's model has shown us how to ask and receive more than we ask for. God is able to do exceedingly abundantly above what we ask nor think according to the power that works in us **(Ephesians 3:20)**.

1. Solomon acknowledge, magnified, and reverenced the Lord **(1 Kings 3:6)**.
2. He humbled himself before the Lord.
3. He was people oriented in his prayers.
4. He sought for the progress of the people of God (The Kingdom).

Are you selfishly asking God to bless you? Why do you seek for the blessing? Why are you asking for that healing? Why do you want those children? Why are you looking for that spouse? Why do you want that expansion? Why do you want to prosper? What are you seeking for peace and joy? What is the reason behind your asking for that blessing?

If you want God to be pleased with your prayers and grant your heart's desire and add exceedingly abundantly above what you ask for, then seek first the kingdom, seek to be a blessing to your world, seek to be a sign and a wonder leading many to Christ with your health and wealth **(Matthew 6:33)**. Let what you are looking for be a testimony that will bring joy to many and put smiles on people's faces.

If you ask for financial blessings just to satisfy your selfish desires, you will get them in trickles. Ask for good health, so you can be a blessing to people, ask for children so they can be raised for God, ask for a husband/wife, so you can walk together to bless the world and raise godly children who will take over the world for Christ. Ask for expansion, so that men will be blessed. Be people-oriented and kingdom focused in all you ask for. Solomon had more than what he asked for because he sought first the kingdom (Matthew 6:33). Change your pattern of prayer and God will be pleased with you and send more than enough your way.

The good news is someone's "exceeding-abundantly blessing" is sent already. All you need is to ask, and it is released into your hands this week. God is saying to someone, "Ask what I shall give you". There is an open cheque awaiting you. However, you need to ask wisely to receive it.

PRAYER: Father, thank you for your word. We pray like the disciples, "Lord, teach us how to pray ", we are tired of asking for one thing for weeks, months, years without answers. Open the heavens and give us an understanding heart that we might receive all our accrued blessings. Thank you, Lord, for answers, in Jesus' name.

Day 4

Don't Rush, Wait!

Bible Reading: Habakkuk 2:1

"I will stand upon my watch, and set me upon the tower, and will watch to see what he will say unto me, and what I shall answer when I am reproved" **(Habakkuk 2:1).**

Good morning, Family of the On-time God. He is ever faithful. His mercy is from everlasting to everlasting, hallelujah!

Brethren, God's plans for us are plans of good and not of evil to give us a future and a hope and bring us to an expected end **(Jeremiah 29:11)**. However, man tends to hurry to achieve and accomplish his heart's desire without the input of the One with the blueprint. Before building a house, an architect prepares its design/plan, forming the basis for the building of the edifice. Having the money, materials, and artisans available on site is insufficient to begin building. The architect with the building plan must be present to build as specified by the owner and deliver as expected at the end. Likewise, we must wait for the architect of our life to fulfil our destiny as desired.

Why are you in a hurry when you have not received direction from God? Why are you frustrated when you have not sought His plan for your life? Why are you hopeless when you have not wait-ed for Him to show you your destiny? Some of us are in a hurry to start "our building" without a plan and the Planner. Where are you going? When are you to leave? What and who do you need on that journey? What does God expect at the end? What is your set goal? Some of us cannot answer any of these. What are you seeing? For as far as your eye can see will be given to you. Are we just following the path that everyone is going? Are you following the plan and the expectation of man for your lives?

God never rushed to create the earth. He brooded over the face of the deep before he began to create **(Genesis 1:2)**. Moses rushed to deliver an Israelite, but God had to take him to Midian to teach him how to wait for instruction **(Exodus 2, 3)**. Are you rushing into your day, marriage, business, relationship, ministry, or job? Are you jumping to conclusions without the architect of your life? Are you complaining about where He is taking you to without going to Him to show you why He is taking you that way? You need to call the architect of your life and destiny daily for direction and interpretation of His plan for your life.

Brethren, there is an expected end, and it is a good end for you if you follow His plan **(Jeremiah 29:11, 1 Corinthians 2:9)**. The good news for someone today is that God will release his plans to you as you stand upon your watch. He will open your understanding to SEE what He has to SAY. He will terminate your confusion and give you a definite direction and instructions. Today, the Lord shall show you a way out of your challenges.

PRAYER: *Father, thank you for your word. We repent for rushing. We pray that you redirect our steps out of the traps we had unknowingly entered. Please show us the way out of our present challenge, teach us to wait on you each day, lead us in the way we should go, and bring us to our desired haven, in Jesus' name.*

Day 5

Go Back and Build Up Your Ruins

Bible Reading: Joshua 8:1-3, 28

> *"And the LORD said unto Joshua, Fear not, neither be thou dismayed: take all the people of war with thee, and arise, go up to Ai: see, I have given into thy hand the king of Ai, and his people, and his city, and his land"* **(Joshua 8:1).**

Good morning, Family of Jehovah Nissi, He is the Almighty, hallelujah!

Brethren, life is full of mountains and valleys, battles to fight, and victories to obtain. Sometimes temporary defeat is experienced by the children of God. However, He told us never to give up because He had won the victory already for His children. The children of Israel lost the battle to Ai due to the sin of Achan. Ai rejoiced because they defeated Israel, whom the people feared because of God's mighty works in their midst. However, they never knew that our God never loses battles.

After Achan's destruction, God sent back Joshua to revisit the ruins, return to fight, and gain the victory originally kept for them. Joshua arose, went back to the battle, and utterly destroyed Ai and gained victory over the city that defeated them. Do you have any Ai (Ruin) in your life? Do you have any battles you fought, and it seemed you were defeated? Did you throw in the towel because of the shame of the last defeat? Did you feel as though God had failed you? Locate that "Achan" in your life, deal with it, go back to Ai, and destroy it forever.

God is sending this word to someone, "Fear not, neither be thou dismayed: take all the people of war with thee, and arise, go up to Ai: see, I have given into thy hand the king of Ai, and his people, and his city, and his land." Get up, put on your strength, quit yourself as men, and go back and fight for your inheritance. Go back and possess your possession. The light affliction was for a moment. See the victory ahead of you and step out and defeat those enemies who defeated you. Joshua did, Nehemiah did, and you can do it also. The God of Joshua is also your God.

Fear not! You have all it takes to defeat your adversary!

PRAYER: *Father, thank you for your word. Empower us to go back and revisit our ruins, restore all that had been stolen, confiscated, and delayed from us, and give us victory over our perpetual enemies in Jesus' name.*

Day 6

Divine Acceleration

Bible Reading: 1 Kings 18:41-46

"And the hand of the LORD was on Elijah; and he girded up his loins, and ran before Ahab to the entrance of Jezreel" **(1 Kings 18:46).**

Good morning, Family of the God of Wonders, He is the same yesterday, today, and forever, hallelujah!

Brethren, stagnation, and delays are enemies of progress. Some have stagnated for years, they have moved so slowly in their life's journey, and the devil has hindered them so that they have nothing to propel them forward to accomplish their goals. However, there is provision for speed for every child of God in the place of prayer.

Elijah went up to the mountain to pray and release rain that the Lord held back for three and a half years. He prevailed in the place of prayer. The rain clouds gathered, but something else happened to him: "the hand of the Lord came upon him" he gained speed to accelerate, out-ran Ahab's chariot, and speedily got to his destination.

Jesus took his disciples to pray on the mountain. As he prayed, suddenly, he transfigured (i.e., transformed into something more beautiful or elevated) **(Mark 9:2-30)**. The disciples, amid the storm, be-came so afraid, but when Jesus came into their boat, they were immediately at the shore **(John 6:21)**. Abraham's eldest servant prayed, saying, "Lord, send me good speed this day... "And before he had done speaking, Rebekah came out" **(Genesis 24:12-15)**.

What have you been dragging along with you? What has stagnated in your life and has been delayed for years? Speed can be in-creased in the place of prayer. The hand of the Lord can be upon you as you pray. You can suddenly be transfigured as you pray. You gain speed of accomplishment in the place of prayer. God can suddenly transform your life as His hand comes upon you. You can outrun those that left you behind.

Go up to the mountain and pray. Bring Jesus into your boat! The good news is that the God of Abraham, Elijah, and the disciples of Jesus Christ is still the same yesterday, today, and forever. Today, you will accelerate to high speeds. You will awake from your prison and sleep in the palace. God will suddenly transform your life. Stagnation is over in your life today. Your challenge will lose his address suddenly. The Egyptian you saw yesterday would suddenly be no more for-ever.

PRAYER: *Father, thank you for your word. Let your hand come mightily upon us, send us good speed, transform everyone, and let us immediately get to our shores, in Jesus' name.*

Day 7

Hidden by God, Not Forgotten

Bible Reading: Exodus 2:1-9

"And the woman conceived and bare a son: and when she saw him that he was a goodly child, she hid him three months" **(Exodus 2:2).**

Good morning, Family of the All-wise God, He is marvellous in His ways, Hallelujah to the Lord!

Brethren, a hiding place in God is the safest place you can be. God sometimes hides his children from calamities and troubles, but our inability to discern times and seasons in our lives robs us of the peace we are to experience when we are in his pavilion (the hiding place of God) **(Psalms 27:5).**

Jochebed, the mother of Moses, discerned that the baby Moses was a goodly child (a child of destiny) and decided to hide him from trouble, from the sword of Pharaoh until the appointed time for him to be taken to Pharaoh's house. God's hand was behind each of the scenes **(Exodus 2).**

Jochebed prepared the ark and placed him among the flags by the river's brink.

Moses was left all alone. He would have asked: Why did my mother do this? Why did everyone abandon me in the cold? I am left alone to die; my end has come; where are the comfort and the love and attention, I used to enjoy from everyone? What did I do wrong to deserve this? However, he was not abandoned; he was being watched over by Mariam, his elder sister, awaiting his elevation to being a 'prince of Egypt.'

Have you ever felt all alone? Have you ever felt abandoned, forgotten, side-lined, unnoticed? You are not forgotten but hidden from trouble until the time of your showing forth. John was hidden in the wilderness until the time of his showing forth **(Luke 1:80)**. Joseph was taken from the environment of his wicked brothers and hidden in Potiphar's house and the prison in Egypt until the time of his showing forth **(Psalms 105:17-20)**. God hid David in the bush until the time of his showing forth **(1 Samuel 17)**. Jesus' star was hidden from the eyes of the wise men to preserve him from the sword of Herod. He was hidden in a manger and also in Egypt until the time of his showing forth **(Matthew 2)**.

There is pain, tears, and the feeling of being hated and abandoned in your hiding place. However, knowing who has placed you in your hiding place, awareness of what you are hidden from, and the glory set before you will keep you rejoicing even when you feel all alone. Joseph's countenance was not sad; David increased his intimacy with God, and John developed his gifts in the wilderness that later attracted men to him in that wilderness.

What are you indulged in at your hiding place? Do you spend your time gripping, weeping, complaining, wishing that you should die or move out? Cheer up! Your hiding place is your place of preparation, increased intimacy with God, building capacity to fly, storing energy for your assignment ahead, and preparing for the glory ahead. It is a school of humility. Moses was not forgotten or abandoned by the river's brink; his sister still watched him. You are not forgotten; you are not abandoned. God has sent angels to watch over you in your hiding place **(Psalms 91:11)**. You are not alone; Jesus can never leave or forsake you **(Hebrew 13:5)**. Pharaoh's daughter noticed Moses. David was sent for and anointed king. Joseph was sent for and appointed a prime minister. John was shown forth to Israel as a great prophet. The wise men noticed Jesus' star again, and the angel of the Lord spoke to Joseph (The Husband of Mary) to return Jesus to Israel. Just as these came to pass, so shall your time of showing forth come.

What do you do in your hiding place?

1. Keep joy alive.
2. Let peace reign in your heart.
3. Build intimacy with God (give yourself to study and pray).
4. Be rest assured that the day of your showing forth is coming.
5. Keep your hope alive.

The good news is your day of hiding is over. Heaven has declared your day of your showing forth. You will be remembered in His hiding place, the 'king' will send for you, and you will no longer be hidden. Your time of glory has come.

Arise and shine!

PRAYER: *Father, thank you for your word. Let the king send for us, showcase us to our world as a desirable finished product. Keep us hidden from the eyes of our adversaries until the time of our showing forth, keep us away from murmuring and complaining, and give us an understanding heart and a discerning spirit to know our times and seasons. Keep us intimate with you perpetually, in Jesus' name.*

Day 8

Fear Not! It Is a Vain Counsel

Bible Reading: Psalms 2:1-5

"Why do the heathen rage and the people imagine a vain thing?"
(Psalms 2:1).

Good morning, Family of the Most-High God, His faithfulness is forever, hallelujah!

Brethren, wickedness is real, evil imagination is real, but even more real is the saving hands of our God. You do not need to offend anyone for him to hate you, nor step on any toe for the enemy to try to strike you. The truth is that the devil, the father of all the agents of darkness on the earth, hates you because you belong to God. He is envious of you because you took his place in heaven as a worshipper of our God, and God's love for man is unfathomable. However, God classifies all their imaginations as 'vain thing.'

What is a vain thing or counsel? Vain is defined as producing no result, useless, unsuccessful, futile, pointless, or having no sense. It, therefore, means that all the scheming and counsels against you, your family, business, job, wife, husband, children, health, finances, ministry, and your life generally is useless, pointless, futile, vain, nonsense, unsuccessful!!!

What did God say concerning you?

1. They shall surely gather but not by me. Anyone that gathers against you shall fall for your sake **(Isaiah 54:15)**.
2. Whosoever digs a pit shall fall into it **(Proverbs 26:27)**.
3. They shall come in one way but flee in seven ways **(Deuteronomy 28:7)**.
4. No weapon formed against you shall prosper **(Isaiah 54:17)**.
5. And whoever falls on this stone will be broken; but on whomever it falls, it will grind him to powder" **(Matthew 21:44)**.
6. Anyone that touches you touches the apple of God's eye **(Zechariah 2:8)**.
7. I will be an enemy to your enemy and an adversary to your adversary **(Exodus 23:23)**.
8. They shall eat up their flesh and drink their blood **(Isaiah 49:26)**.
9. Take counsel together; it shall not stand **(Isaiah 8:10)**.
10. The Lord is my shield and buckler **(Psalms 18:2)**.
11. The angel of the Lord encamps round about them that fear Him and delivers them **(Psalms 34:7)**.
12. Surely there is no enchantment against Jacob, neither is there any divination against Israel **(Numbers 23:23)**.
13. I will build my church, and the gate of hell cannot prevail against it **(Matthew 16:18)**.

Are you still in doubt that all the devil's scheming is vain? All their counsel is futile because the Lord is our rock, and He is jealous over His own. Pharaoh tried it and drowned in the red sea **(Exodus 14)**. The people of mount Seir, Moab, and Ammon tried it, and they helped to kill one another **(1 Chronicles 20)**. Daniel's colleagues tried it, and the lions licked every drop of their blood and flesh **(Daniel 6)**. Haman tried it and saw his last hours on the earth on the gallows he prepared for Mordecai **(Esther 7)**. Judas tried it and ended up committing suicide **(Matthew 27)**.

Fear not! All the gang-up of hell against your life and destiny is vain; it cannot stand. The God of yesterday is still the same today. His word stands forever. He cannot change or alter the things that come from His mouth. However, God has shown us how to deal with the devil and his plans. The Bible says, "He that sits in the heavens shall laugh and shall speak to them in His sore displeasure" **(Psalms 2)**.

Are you closing your mouth? A closed mouth is a closed destiny! Begin to speak against your adversary, declare their counsel futile, and decree their activity an exercise in futility. What adversities are you experiencing? Open your mouth and declare that sickness, marital delays, pain, poverty, jobless-ness, threatened marital break, challenges with your children, unemploy-ment, attack on your ministry and church, home, business, etc., futile, unsuccessful, and nonsense! As you say it, you will see it.

The good news is it is well with you. No weapon formed against you shall prosper. Every tongue that rises against you in judgment is condemned. You shall rise above every scheming of the devil over your life and come out victorious.

PRAYER: *Father, thank you for your word. Arise, Oh Lord, and silence every voice revolting against us, have in derision all that take counsel against our life and destiny. Give us peace on every side in Jesus' name.*

Day 9

Get Out of Your Comfort Zone

Bible Reading: Genesis 12:1-3

"Get thee out of thy country, and from thy kindred and from thy father's house unto a land that I will show you" **(Genesis 12:1).**

Good morning, Family of the Covenant-Keeping God. He is faithful, hallelujah!

Brethren, a comfort zone is a situation where one feels safe or at ease. It is also a settled method of working that requires little effort and yields only barely acceptable results. There is no room for improvement in a comfort zone. God needed Abraham to be blessed, to become great. He had great things in store for him. However, He could not achieve these things while still in his father's house. His mindset had to be transformed; his values had to be improved; his horizon had to be widened; his mind had to be renewed.

God sent him out to release the blessing initially kept for him before the foundation of the world. Are you still in your comfort zone, carrying about the same mindset? Are you still going about in circles, doing the same things, having the same thoughts, meeting the same people, staying on the same horizon, and expecting to go forward and improve in your business, job, ministry, family, and life generally?

You can't access that level of blessing if you do not get out of your norms. Step out and think outside the box. Be transformed by renewing your mind, do something new; meet new people. Get new challenges and conquer new territories. Abraham departed from his everyday lifestyle, out of the mindset of his father's house, and became great and blessed in all things **(Genesis 24:1)**.

The good news today is that you will contact your blessings as you get out of your comfort zone. The word of God will transform your mind and take you to a new horizon where you will access your victories, wealth, and wholeness. Get out and get blessed.

PRAYER: *Father, thank you for your word. Hold our hands and lead us to our place of blessings. Help us out of our comfort zone so that we might become a blessing to our world. Release your blessings in abundance to us by your word today, in Jesus' name.*

Day 10

Make It Happen; Be Specific

Bible Reading: Mark 10:46-52

"And Jesus answered and said unto him, What wilt thou that I should do unto thee? The blind man said unto him, Lord, that I might receive my sight" (Mark 10:51).

Good morning, Family of the Compassionate God, His mercy endures forever.

Brethren, God is in the business of changing lives, healing the sick, setting the captives free, wiping away tears from the eyes of men, and answering prayers. However, for some, their answers are far-fetched because they ask amiss. Bartimaeus, the blind man who sat by the highway, received his sight instantly. Jesus, in his healing, gave us the key to the speedy answer to prayers. Jesus saw that he had faith, but his prayer was not specific.

Bartimaeus was ready to be healed. He had gathered information about the healing power of Jesus, went after Jesus, and cried out for help but missed it all. He did not get healed because he only cried out and called the name of Jesus. His prayer was, "have mercy upon me." Jesus stood still, called for him, and told him how to receive what he needed. Jesus asked, "What do you really want me to do for you?" (Paraphrased).

Many have prayed, cried, fasted, and prayed for blessings, change of story, and healing but are not specific in their request. They have prayed for the blessings of the Lord in their lives and have seen no changes. They have missed it in the place of prayers. If you want the hand of God to act speedily in your life, be specific, and ask for the exact thing you are looking for. Hannah asked for a male child, and she got Samuel, Bartimaeus asked for his sight, and he received it, Solomon asked for wisdom to lead Israel, and he received it. What do you really want? Have a target, don't just throw stones in all directions. Sit down, prepare your specific needs, go to God in faith, and like Bartimaeus, you will return with all your answers.

The good news is that Jesus is asking you the same question "What will you have me do for you?". He is the same yesterday, today, and forever. You will doubtless return with testimonies in your hands.

PRAYER: *Father, thank you for your word. Do unto us as you did to Bartimaeus, teach us how to receive from you speedily. Answer all our prayers of specific needs in Jesus' name.*

Day 11

Posted to Destiny

Bible Reading: Genesis 37:18-28

"Come now therefore, and let us slay him, and cast him into some pit, and we will say, some evil beast hath devoured him: and we shall see what will become of his dreams" **(Genesis 37:20).**

Good morning, Family of the Covenant-Keeping God. He is faithful, hallelujah!

Brethren, the whole world lies in wickedness **(1 John 5:19)**. The devil hates you with a passion, and he uses human agents upon the earth to exhibit his depth of hatred to mar your glorious destiny in God. However, God Almighty loves you more and watches over His plan for you up to fulfilment. He turns the enemy's plan in your favour and makes the diviners mad **(Isaiah 44:25)**. What a mighty God we serve!

Joseph, hated by his brother, had a glorious destiny, revealed to him in dreams. His brothers conspired (took counsel) together to destroy him and end his destiny. However, He that sitteth in the heavens laughed **(Psalms 2:1-2)**. He turned their counsel in favour of Joseph. He got posted to Egypt to meet with destiny. They thought they had quenched his dream, that it was all over for Joseph. They thought they had finished with him, but God turned it for his good.

David was sent to the bush to tend "those little sheep" the brothers thought He was very proud of. They thought they could quench his destiny, but God located him in the bush and took him from the bush to the palace **(1 Samuel 17:28)**.

Solomon was side-lined and disregarded. The son of Bathsheba, wife of Uriah, was forgotten and rejected by his brethren, not called to the get-together of all his brethren, but God called him from that corner and put him on the throne **(1 Kings 1:1-40)**.

Jesus, the son of God, was betrayed and killed to end his existence on the earth, but if they had known, they wouldn't have crucified the King of glory. God gave him a name above all names and crowned him with glory. He became the King of kings, the Lord of lords, and the head of all principalities and powers **(John 11:50, 1 Corinthians. 2:8, Philippians 2:9-13)**.

Are you rejected, side-lined, disregarded, forsaken, posted to an unknown destination, stripped of your beauty and honour, made to be nothing? Has the devil posted you (son of Abraham of God) to a place of dishonour, a pit of dryness, a place of slavery, a prison yard, or the bush?

Rejoice, for you are on your way to your throne. Have you not heard that the stone the builders rejected has become the chief cornerstone? **(Psalms 118:22)**. Have you not heard that He turned the counsel of Ahithophel to foolishness? **(2 Samuel 17:1-29)**. Have you not heard that He makes all things work together for good to them that love Him and are called according to his purpose? **(Romans 8:28)**.

Cheer up, child of God. It is not the end of your story. Being pushed aside, forgotten, or disregarded is often a pathway to greatness. Cheer up! Praise (Judah) amid your challenges will post you to your destined location. You are a king and a priest, your place in destiny nobody can occupy. Your destiny, no one can thwart. For when God speaks, everything hears and will align themselves to His plan, and your end shall be as expected **(Genesis 24:1)**. As the delays and troubles in the life of Joseph did not stop him from ascending his throne, your throne also will be occupied by you.

The good news is that your destiny is preserved for you, your throne no one can take. Your posting will end with you on your throne, in Jesus' name.

PRAYER: *Father, thank you, for we know you are in charge, and nothing can stop us. We surrender everything to you, hold our hands, and lead us safely to our thrones, in Jesus' name.*

Day 12

Your Victory Is Not in Numbers but in God

Bible Reading: 1 Chronicles 21:1-7

"And God was displeased with this thing; therefore, He smote Israel" **(1 Chronicles 21:7).**

Good morning, Family of the Jealous God. His love is everlasting, hallelujah!

Brethren, pride goes before a fall. Every pride has the backing of the devil with an intention to destroy. David counted the people of Israel, concentrating on his mighty army. Why did he do this against the counsel of Joab?

1. Pride.
2. To know his achievements.
3. To gauge the strength of his army.

God was displeased with him because He was about to sing his own praise, shifting his trust in God to the strength of his army and becoming proud. He was able to unite Israel and Judah to fight battles.

Brethren, you do not need to count numbers; what you have in your bank account, what you possess in the house, the strength of the people you have, the number of influential friends or family members you know. God is more than able to do more than your numbers. He does not depend on your strength or numbers to win your battles. He does not depend on your strength or how many people you know to secure you that job. He does not rely on numbers (amount) to provide for you and your family.

Gideon's army was reduced from 32,000 to 300, but he still won the battle **(Judges 7)**. The woman of Zarephath had only a handful of meal and a little oil, but God still fed them all through the famine **(1 Kings 17:7-16)**. The wife of the prophet had only a jar of oil but still became an oil merchant **(2 Kings 4)**. Jesus had only 2 fishes and 5 loaves of bread, yet He still fed 5,000 **(Matthew 14:13-21)**. Why is your heart troubled when you see a decrease in your storehouse, your bank account, your possessions? Could it be that your trust is not absolutely in God but in your possessions? Take your mind off numbers; trust in God. He is more than able to do exceedingly abundantly above what you ask or say **(Ephesians 3:20)**. Trusting in numbers will displease God, bring pride, and invite punishment upon the people.

Woe unto them that put their trust in man or in princes. Nebuchadnezzar began to count his achievements, and he was reduced to a beast **(Daniel 4:28-35)**. David counted Israel, and the people were destroyed **(1 Chronicles 21:1-14)**. Get up, stop the calculations, be anxious for nothing, give God praise and thanks, and all your heart desires shall be granted.

The good news is, it is not by power nor by might but by the workings of the Spirit of the Lord **(Zechariah 4:6)**. The weapons of our warfare are not carnal but are mighty through God **(2 Corinthians 10:4)**. God shall supply all your needs according to His riches in glory by Christ Jesus **(Philippians 4:19)**. GOD IS ABLE!!!

PRAYER: *Father, thank you for your word. Enable us to trust absolutely in you. Forgive all our sins of unbelief, anxiety, and fear for the future. Provide for all our physical and spiritual needs by Christ Jesus, in the name of Jesus Christ.*

Day 13

God's Word Is All You Need

Bible Reading: Psalms 107:17-22

"He sent his word and healed them and delivered them out of their destructions" **(Psalms 107:20)**.

Good morning, Family of the WORD of God. He is mighty to save, hallelujah!

Brethren, God honours His word above His name **(Psalms 138:2)**. All creations came into being by His word. Nothing made was not made by His word **(John 1:3)**. It, therefore, means that the world without the word is a crumbling world, full of crisis. Chaos, formlessness, darkness, and voidness can be dealt with by His word **(Genesis 1:1-3)**. A challenge of long continuance can be dealt with by His sent word **(Luke 1:13)**. Many run from pillar to post because they are void of the word that deals with their challenges, a word that will turn their situations around. They have prayed all manner of prayers, complained, murmured, cried, and told God all about their challenges, but their cries lack the word in it. Their spirit is empty of the word for the said challenge. What did God say concerning that situation? God said, come to me with strong reasons **(Isaiah 41:21)**. Take with you words and go and pray **(Hosea 14:2)**. A cry without the word is like starting a fire without the wood. The sent word terminates barrenness **(Genesis 21:1)**, dryness **(Ezekiel 37)**, poverty **(Philippians 4:19)**, sickness **(Psalms 107:20)**, change of story **(Genesis 12:1-3)**, healing **(Acts 10:38)**, deliverance **(Mark 16:9)**, victory **(2 Chronicles 20:15-22)**, freedom from prison **(Acts 12:3-19)**, wisdom, abundance, house **(1 Kings 16:9)**, money **(Matthew, 17:24-26)**, growth, etc. The sent word can get all.

Are you downcast, in tears, do you lack direction, facing shame and reproach, embattled, imprisoned by circumstances? Go for the word. Hannah encountered the sent word, and Samuel came forth. Sarah encountered the sent word, and Isaac came; Lazarus encountered the sent word, and death was defeated; Israel encountered the word, and famine was defeated; Saul encountered the word, and his life was changed. A dark world encountered the word and light, and all creations came.

God is still speaking today. He is still changing the stories of men. He is still sending His word to individuals, families, churches, businesses, marriages, and homes today. God is still fixing broken hearts, setting captives free, and winning battles and wars for men today. Are you ready for your own word today? Sit with the word, and you will stop wandering around with your challenges! You are healed, you are delivered, you are saved, you are lifted, your barns are full, and your storehouse is filled, you are a joyful mother of children, you are favoured, you are married, your peace is like a river, you are loved, His presence has returned to you, you have direction.

PRAYER: *Father, we thank you for your word. We pray that we will hear you when you speak. I pray for our faith to receive the sent word, confirm every word sent to us today, and we will return to you with thanksgiving and praises forever, in Jesus' name.*

Day 14

Your Lockdown Is Over

Bible Reading: Exodus 12:1-2

"And the LORD spake unto Moses and Aaron in the land of Egypt, saying, This month shall be your beginning of months; it shall be the first month of the year to you" **(Exodus 12:1-2).**

Good morning, Family of the Deliverer, His outstretched arms turn things around, hallelujah!

Brethren, everything upon the earth that has a beginning has an end. Surely, there is an end, and thy expectation shall not be cut off **(Proverbs 23:18)**.

The children of Israel entered Egypt, and in the process of time, they were enslaved, in bondage, in pain, in agony, in fear of their taskmasters, working much and gaining nothing, under a heavy burden. They cried, but there was no one to save them from the hands of their taskmasters. It seemed hopeless; it seemed God had forgotten Israel in their bondage.

They cried for a deliverer for centuries to no avail. Why Lord! Why are we going through all these, and you do not see?

Suddenly, God came down at the appointed time with His mighty outstretched arms. He sent His word through a deliverer, Moses, and their bondage, imprisonment, and slavery came to an end **(Exodus 3:3-22)**. The time of the plagues in Egypt was over, the time for the children of Israel to leave honourably came, and nothing could stop the release of Israel from this long bondage. The Pharaoh released their children, wives, husbands, businesses, ministries, and everything as they so desired. He made the children of Israel go free out of bondage with great riches, silver, and gold, in haste **(Exodus 12:35-36)**.

Have you been locked down, locked out, cast down, in pain, under taskmasters? Has your business, ministry, children, health, marriage, and life been locked down? Have you been tied down going round in circles for as long as you can remember? Have you been restricted and confined to a corner, alienated from the commonwealth of Zion by the powers of darkness? Have you shed tears both hidden and in the open? Have you been a thing of ridicule or pity that no responsibility is given to you, not because you are not responsible but because the circumstances surrounding you had belittled you?

Cheer up! The Deliverer is here, hallelujah! Sing for joy this month, for the Lion of Judah has prevailed. Pharaoh's tenure is over in your affairs. He is defeated, and his pomp has deflated. In shame, he will let you go in haste. I come with this good news today, "This month shall be the beginning of months for you. Arise and go forth out of your bondage; you, your children, your flocks, your herds, your businesses, your ministry, your marriage, your job, and whatever constitutes your life. Your lockdown is over. And as you go, you shall not go empty, but with gold and silver. You shall not leave your prison empty, but yours shall be with great riches. You shall empty out the enemy, and their wealth shall be transferred to you. What affects others is not permitted to affect you. Your case is different. Congrats, brethren, you have made it to a month of new beginnings, a month of liberation from bondage, a month of breaking limits and limitations!

PRAYER: *Father, we join our voices together to say THANK YOU, LORD, for your word, preservation, protection, and provision. Thank you for coming down to deliver us out of bondage into our liberty at last. We love you, our father, receive all the glory, for breaking the gates of brass, and cutting the bars of iron in sunder in lives. Thank you, Lord, in Jesus' name.*

Day 15

You Are God's Battle Axe

Bible Reading: Jeremiah 51:20

"Thou art my battle axe and weapons of war: for with thee will I break in pieces the nations, and with thee will I destroy kingdoms" **(Exodus 12:1-2).**

Good morning, Family of the God of War, He is the Almighty! Hallelujah!

What is a battle axe? A battle axe is a specially designed weapon used in battles against the enemy, capable of destroying even the armoured foe. God is a Warrior God, and from generation to generation, He works with man to showcase His power on the earth. He used Moses against Pharaoh **(Exodus 5).** He used David against the giant Goliath **(1 Kings 17).** He used Elijah to destroy the prophets of Baal **(1 Kings 18:20-40).** He used Joshua against the Amalekites **(Exodus 17:8).** He used Peter against the magician **(Acts 8:9-24).** God seeks to use you to break down kingdoms, destroy the works of the enemies, and bring down the edifice built by the enemy in your life.

It is one thing to be a battle-axe; it is another to be fit for the master's use. Every battle-axe that qualifies to be taken into the battlefield must be:

1. Sharp
2. Strong
3. Powerful
4. Easily available
5. Must not be rusted

The word of God is the file of your spirit. Being empty of the word of God is being blunt in the battles of life **(2 Timothy 2:15, Luke 4:4)**. Jesus defeated the devil in the desert with the word of God. The word countered the devil's arrows. Sharpen your axe head today. No warrior will take a weak, unreliable, axe into the enemy's camp to defend himself. A weak axe in the hand of a warrior is a sure way to be defeated. God expects us to be strong in the face of battles. Those that do know their God (the word) shall be strong and shall do exploit **(Daniel 11:32)**. An axe must be powerful. We have received the power and authority (Acts 1:8) to trample upon Satan. Are you exercising this authority? The more we exercise it, the more confident we will be to face fiercer battles. Spiritual warfare must not be fought with rusted weapons. What constitutes this rust?

Lack of use, addiction to food, drinks, sleep, and other idols in our lives. They that wait on the Lord shall renew their strength **(Isaiah 40:31)**. Addiction to food and drinks makes a weak spirit. Food made Adam lose the battle over his enemy, the devil **(Genesis. 3:6-8)**, but Jesus came, fasted to receive spiritual strength, and defeated the devil **(Luke 4:1-13)**. Are you ready for a victorious life? Are you ready to be more than a conqueror? Then this good news is for you. "You are His battle axe; you have laid dormant and ignorant of who you are. With you will I break in pieces those mountains before you, those long-lasting challenges will become as nothing".

Get up! Make yourself available for the master's use. You have watched the enemy challenge you these 40 days. It's time to pick up your stones, sling, and face the devil. The bragging of the enemy cannot stop if the "David" in you will not rise. Fear not. You are His battle axe. Go fight again with the knowledge of who you are in God.

PRAYER: *Father, thank you for your word. Please give us the strength to prepare ourselves for life's battles. As a warrior sharpens and lubricates his axe for battle, sharpen us and anoint us afresh for the battles of life. Give us victory at last, in Jesus' name.*

Day 16

Wise Men Give Praise

Bible Reading: Psalms 107:8

"Oh that men would praise the Lord for his goodness, and for his wonderful works to the children of men!" **(Psalms 107:8).**

Good morning, Family of the Wonder-Working God, His wonders are unfathomable, hallelujah!

Brethren, wise men, observe God's wonders and praise Him **(Psalm 107:43)**. How many times have you cried in distress, and the Lord appeared at the scene and solved those problems, wiped away your tears and set you free? How often have you looked everywhere for help, and suddenly help is sent to you while you are still speaking? It was not that human agent used; it was God! It was not that human agent used; it was God!

How many times have you sinned against the Lord and cried to him, and He forgave you? It was not because you know how to cry; it was Jesus!

How many times have you disregarded Him and murmured against His will, but He still forgave you and brought you to your desired haven? It was His Love! How many times have you been hungry, and He fed you, sick and He healed you; lost and not finding your way and He found you; wandered in the wilderness and He brought you to your Canaan? It was not your strength and wisdom. It was God! Oh, that men would praise the Lord for His goodness and for his wonderful works to the children of men!

The Bible says, *"If you will not hear, and if you will not take it to heart, to give glory to My name," Says the LORD of hosts, "I will send a curse upon you, And I will curse your blessings. Yea, I have cursed them already, because you do not take it to heart"* **(Malachi 2:2)**. Jesus asked, *"Were there not ten cleansed, where are the nine?"* **(Luke 17:17)**.

Many have lost their blessings to ungratefulness. Many have attributed their success to their hard work and consistency only. Some have boasted of their qualifications and educational background for those jobs and promotions. Some have given glory to their fathers, uncles, relations, or friends for those daily provisions. Some have thought their righteousness had brought them to the level of blessings they have received daily. Lie! That is the trick of the devil to rob you of more blessings and place you under the curse of God. Ungratefulness is a sin of omission that attracts God's curses and brings stagnation to men **(Malachi. 2:2)**.

Remember, Nebuchadnezzar!!! SELAH! Wise men, observe the blessings of the Lord, both "big" and "small", and give all the glory back to the Doer. Praisers multiply; ungrateful men diminish! Which of these are you? SELAH!

PRAYER: *Father, thank you for this word. I choose to praise you all the days of my life and return the glory to your name. We have returned to thank you for life, peace, children, marriages,* *jobs, provision, preservation, protection, healings, forgiveness, answers to prayers, chastening, corrections, encouragements, your daily word, instructions, prophecies, breakthrough, our home, growth, expansions, pauses, elevations, mountains, valleys, your word. We can't name all you have done, but we shout, Hallelujah to you, Oh Lord! in Jesus' name.*

Day 17

The Touch of Faith

Bible Reading: Luke 8:45

"And Jesus said, "Who touched Me?" When all denied it, Peter and those with him said, "Master, the multitudes throng and press You, and You say, 'Who touched Me?'" **(Luke 8:45).**

Good morning, Family of God, He is mighty to save, hallelujah!

Brethren, there is power in Jesus. He is the power and wisdom of God. In Him dwells the Godhead bodily. All power in heaven, on earth, and underneath the earth had been given unto him. He is the Word of God, the Creator of all things. He heals the sick, sets the captives free, feeds the hungry, and wipes away tears. He raises the dead, lifts the poor from the dunghill, and makes them sit with the princes of the land. He heals the broken hearted, delivers the captives, sets at liberty those bruised, battered, and beaten by circumstances, heals homes, and changes stories of men in a twinkling of an eye. HE IS I AM THAT I AM **(Luke 4:18, Exodus 3:14, John 8: 58).**

There is no argument He is everything, and everything is in Him. Why then do men call, cry, touch, seek, and it seems He cannot be found of them. Why are others coming from the back (new in the kingdom) and getting touched by the Master? Why are they giving great testimonies of deliverance? "Familiarity brings contempt," they say. Are you so familiar with the word that you can no longer draw virtue from Him? Are you so familiar with the word of God that you only see the letter but cannot draw the Rhema/spirit embedded in the word of God?

Are you so familiar with His presence that you cannot draw answers in His presence? Are you so familiar with the mouthpiece of God (His prophets, teachers, apostles, evangelists, and Pastors) that you can no longer draw virtue from the word sent through them?

The town of Jesus could not experience his miracles because they were too familiar with Him **(Matthew 13:58)**. Gehazi forgot that the God that works in His Master is omnipresent and omnipotent; he lost it to carelessness **(2 Kings 5:1-27)**. Jesus' disciples touched Jesus all the days of His life on the earth, but they could not draw virtue from Him. However, the woman came from behind and received her healing because her faith in Jesus was still intact **(Luke 8:48)**. Where is your faith? **(Luke 8:25)**.

Jesus still heals, delivers, saves, mends the broken hearted, sets the captives free, wipes away tears, meets the needs of the needy, is a friend to the friendless, father to the orphans, and husband to the widow. He still multiplies, makes the barren to keep house, puts the solitary in families, He is still, I AM THAT I AM.

Brethren let's go back to our first love and trust in his mighty power; let's resist the temptation to be too familiar with His word and lose out in the blessings He carries. The good news is that He is waiting with open arms for you. If you run to Him, He will run to you. If you lift your hands in faith, He will raise you up. If you call to Him in faith, He will answer you. His love never fails!!!

Day 18

He Hears and Answers

Bible Reading: Luke 18:7

"And shall God not avenge His own elect who cry out day and night to Him, though He bears long with them?" **(Luke 18:7)**.

Good morning, Family of the Rewarder of the Diligent, His mercy endures forever, hallelujah!

Brethren, problems, and challenges don't last forever for the children of God. Weeping may last for the night, but joy comes in the morning. There is time for everything under the earth, time to ask, and time to receive **(Ecclesiastes 3:1)**. The enemy of our soul can only harass us for a season, night seasons can only be for a while, but the morning will soon dawn. Jesus showed in this parable how to persist in your request till you have the answers in your hands. The widow had faith, so she returned to the King severally to ask. She believed beyond doubt that a day would come when her request would be granted **(Luke 18:1-8)**.

Have you asked for "long"? Are you on the verge of your miracle and want to quit? Recently, a 68-year-old woman whose husband is 71 delivered their twins after 40 years of marriage. They never gave up. They held on to the end and had double honour. Don't give up, don't quit, don't through in the towel, don't resign to "fate". Is what you are asking the will of God? **(1 John 5:15-16)**, Is it a good thing? **(James 1:17)**, will it bring glory to the God who promised? **(Isaiah 40:5)**. Did you "see" it for yourself? **(Genesis 13:14-17)**, is your faith secured? **(Luke 18:8)**, was it so from the beginning? **(Matthew 19:4, Genesis 1:26-28, 2:8, 22)**.

Then go on, hold unto His promises, go to Him with words, go day and night. Go to Him with strong reasons, and He will avenge you of all your adversaries and detractors.

He will turn your captivity around, save and deliver you from all your destructions. He will surely avenge all your years of bondage, shame, reproach, disgrace, waiting, and tears. He will put a permanent smile on your face **(Ecclesiastes 3:14)**. Do not quit!!! The good news is, "God shall avenge you of all your adversaries speedily as you approach Him one more time in faith. The days of judgments of all your adversaries have come. Congratulations, victory is finally yours in Jesus' name.

PRAYER: *Father, thank you for your word. We come together and cry to you one more time, "Oh Lord, please avenge us of all our adversaries." Open the files that were closed for years and settle the long-forgotten issues against us this week in Jesus' name.*

Day 19

God Will Turn It Around

Bible Reading: Genesis 18:10

"Is anything too hard for the Lord? At the time appointed I will return unto thee, according to the time of life, and Sarah shall have a son" **(Genesis 18:10).**

Good morning, Family of the Captivity-Turning God. He is the same yesterday, today, forever, hallelujah!

Brethren, Is anything too hard for the Lord? **(Genesis 18:14)**. Sarah laughed in her heart at the word the Angel spoke to Abraham, saying, "Sarah thy wife shall bear thee a son". Do we despise Sarah for doubting the words of this Stranger? All the natural laws of childbearing were against her. It was impossible for that ever to happen again. She had given up hope and decided to move on with her life. She must have thought, "who is this talking, maybe because they have not seen me, they do not know my story".

However, God visited Sarah as He has said; Isaac came at the time appointed by heaven. Their captivity turned around. Suddenly, Abraham and Sarah became the parents of Isaac. It must have looked like a dream. The impossible became a reality because God said it. Is anything too hard for the Lord? Elisha, the prophet of God, said, "Tomorrow by this time, a measure of fine flour shall be sold for a shekel..." **(2 Kings 7:1-20)**. Against all economic and agricultural laws, the famine suddenly became abundant in 24 hours because God said it.

Is anything too hard for the Lord? Jeremiah says, "nothing is too hard for thee" **(Jeremiah 32:17)**. Ponder, meditate upon the answer Jeremiah has given. Declare it to your hearing, let the world hear you, let heavens hear you, let the devil and his agents hear you, NOTHING IS TOO HARD FOR THE LORD!"

The good news is that God will turn your captivity around like a dream in the night. Your story of woes and pain will become history. The problems that defied medical and any human wisdom will suddenly be turned around in your favour because the Lord said so. All your seed sown will doubtless return as sheaves in abundance. All your piled-up prayers, confiscated, stopped, arrested, delayed by the devil, are released. All that accrue to you are released. You shall be a sign and a wonder in this season where the world has been thrown into confusion. You shall doubtless come again rejoicing. Stay ready for God's visitation!!!

PRAYER: *Father, thank you for your word. We believe, receive, and will soon become it. Turn again our captivity as you have said, give us a dream-like turn around today in Jesus' name.*

Day 20

Watch Your Thoughts

Bible Reading: 1 Kings 19:4

"But he himself went a day's journey into the wilderness, and came and sat down under a juniper tree: and he requested for himself that he might die; and said, It is enough; now, O LORD, take away my life; for I am not better than my fathers" (1 Kings 19:4).

Good morning, Family of the Loving Father, His mercy endures forever, hallelujah!

Brethren, your thoughts determine your feelings; your thoughts can also control your actions. Your thoughts can make you confident or bring insecurity; they can create fear or bring boldness. You are controlled by your thoughts; in order words, you are your thoughts. Elijah, a firebrand Prophet of the Most-High God, fled from a woman and requested God to kill him. A man that just called down fire from heaven and slaughtered 450 prophets of Baal ran away from a single woman.

What happened to him? Why did he lose confidence in himself and His God? He thought an evil thought, a thought that was not the truth. He processed what he heard in his mind and lost confidence in his God. He heard that all the prophets were killed, believing it, and meditating on what he heard. Elijah got discouraged and became afraid. He came and sat down under a juniper tree, a tree of fruitfulness, transformation, liberation, and spiritual nourishment and requested to die. But He was wrong. God preserved the seven thousand prophets in the land **(1 Kings 19:18)**.

Watch it; most of what evil things you think of that cause fear and discouragement are false evidence appearing real (F.E.A.R) in your thoughts. God's word concerning you is the only truth. It stands forever. On the other hand, the prodigal son in the pigsty caught a thought, an encouraging thought that propelled him forward to return to his father for restoration. He caught a thought of encouragement, which gave him the courage to approach his father after squandering his wealth **(Luke 15:11-32)**.

What thought have you caught? What have you heard recently? What are you reading lately? What you see or hear forms your thought pattern. What comes as thought will mature into feelings that will birth your behaviours and actions. Be careful, therefore, of what you hear, and see, who you are in contact with, who feeds your mind, and what you feed your mind with. Depressive, discouraging, envy-filled thoughts are formed from what you see or hear. Fear, insecurity, poverty, sickness, success, confidence, health, happiness, love, and hate spring up from your thought and what you meditate or ponder on. Is what is in your thought either discouraging or encouraging?

Watch your thoughts, for as a man thinketh in his heart, so is he **(Proverbs 23:7)**. Do you want to be successful? Be in contact with successful people, anointed books, and videos. Do you want to live a life of thanksgiving? Be around thankful people. Do you want to be joyous? Be around, joyous people. Being in an environment of envious, sad, murmuring, depressed folks affect your thoughts. They feed your thoughts with their wrong words, which, when processed in you, progresses into feelings. Bad company corrupts good manners **(1 Corinthians 15:30)**. Make up your mind today to be transformed in your thought by renewing your mind. Spend time with positive words from God **(Philippians 4:8)**. Watch your thought and guard your heart with all diligence, for out of it are the issues of life **(Proverb 4:2)**.

The good news today is that God has seen you even under that "Juniper tree in your wilderness", He cares for you even in your discouragement. He has baked your 'cake' ready for you. He is ready to take you to the place of truth. So go up to the mountain. Stand there before the Lord; He will give you direction out of discouragement.

PRAYER: *Father, thank you for your word. We can do nothing without you. Please help us renew our minds and restore our confidence in you and your sent word, in Jesus' name.*

Day 21

Watch and Pray

Bible Reading: Matthew 26:41

"Watch and pray that ye enter not into temptation the spirit indeed is willing but the flesh is weak" **(Matthew 26:41)**.

Good morning, Family of the God that sees the end from the beginning. He is the Almighty, hallelujah!

Brethren, the tempter; the devil is more subtle than every creature **(Genesis 3:1)**. He goes about seeking whom he can destroy; therefore, be sober and vigilant **(1 Peter 5:8)**. What are we chasing after? What are we seeking in this world? What are your heart's desires? What is your pressing need for the moment?

Be careful; the tempter crawls in unexpectedly, uninvited. He glides his way in unnoticed. Be vigilant, be sober. How does he come in? He uses the physical senses, gets into your mind, and corrupts it **(Genesis 3)**. He keeps you busy with what is unnecessary and keeps you away from fellowship with your Father. He keeps you engaged with your freshly needs, your ambitions, your jobs, career, or academics, to weaken your source of strength and strikes when you least expect it. He uses the lust of eyes, lust of the flesh and pride of life to get to our minds to corrupt them **(1 John 2:16)**.

Be vigilant, be sober in a bit to gain fame, riches, honour, and meet your physical needs, lest we fall into temptation. The devil deceived Eve because she was not watchful. The devil showed her the beauty of the forbidden fruit, went after God's instruction in her mind, got it corrupted, and caused a fall that cost God His only begotten son.

How do you keep the devil at bay?

Pray: Are you sensing a shift in your belief system? Do you notice that your life tilts more to fleshly activities **(Galatians 5:19-21)** rather than spiritual things **(Galatians 5:22)**? Are you spending more time feeding your physical needs? Are you praying for your will rather than God's in your life? Are you almost giving up on your God-given dreams? Are you spending time comparing yourselves with others? Are you tending to accept the world's view on Christianity? Do you love money more than the Lord? Are you spending more hours on social media than studying the word of God? Are you spending less time in the place of prayer lately? Are you comfortable sitting at home to study the word alone rather than longing for the brethren's assembly? Are you found sleeping more than awake? Is reading/ studying/ praying for an hour an uphill task for you? Are you spending more time arguing about irrelevant things rather than speaking words of wisdom when necessary? Then it's time to pray. These are the signs that the adversary of your soul has begun its strategy to weaken you and get you.

1. Crave to be led by the spirit of the Lord (Romans 8:16).

Whoever you feed more will have the strength to lead you. Being led by the flesh is to succumb to the works of the flesh, leading to destruction. However, being led by the spirit is winning the battles over the devil. Fill your heart with the word of God, and you will not succumb to the will of the flesh.

2. Watch.

Are we living our lives oblivious of the happenings around us? Are we following prophecies and checking what "time" it is we are in. Are we living like the people in the times of Noah, eating, drinking, marrying, and giving to marriage, chasing after money, success, fame and forgetting that we are sojourners here on the earth? Are we living our lives carelessly? Jesus says, "Watch and pray that ye enter not into temptation". What are you praying for? If you do not watch what you are praying for and are not informed, what are you praying for? Are you busy praying for what the prophecies said must come to pass? Watch, study, and get information about what to pray for **(2 Timothy 2:15)**.

3. Use money; don't love money.

The devil rides on the wings of the love of money to deceive many out of the way of truth. The love of money attracts the devil to exhibit his evil plan **(1 Timothy 6:10)**. Money is not your god; it is your servant. By our prosperity shall the gospel be spread abroad. Don't seek to amass wealth for selfish reasons but use it for the furtherance of the kingdom and for helping humanity return to God. The good news today is that Jesus is speaking to someone again: "Come and watch with me this one hour, come and be empowered to deal with the tempter" Watch and pray; the tempter is at hand!!!

PRAYER: *Father, thank you for your warnings today. Empower us with the spirit of grace and supplication, keep the adversary far from our habitation, far from our minds, keep every serpent that comes as a human agent or technological agent away, guide us, and lead us not into temptations. We declare today that we are over-comers in Jesus' name.*

Day 22

Say Not What They Say

Bible Reading: Isaiah 8:12

> *"Say ye not, A confederacy, to all them to whom this people shall say, A confederacy; neither fear ye their fear, nor be afraid"* **(Isaiah 8:12).**

Good morning, Family of the Almighty God who rules over the affairs of men.

Brethren, God is supreme, God is the Governor over all the nations of the earth. He rules over the affairs of men **(Psalm 22:28)**. Nothing happens without his permission; no thought is hidden from Him **(Hebrew 4:13)**. No conspiracy is activated without His knowledge **(Psalms 2)**.

We sometimes forget who God is and we forget who we are in Christ. We are in the world and not of this world; we are from a different kingdom but sent to be kings upon the earth, sent as Ambassadors from the Kingdom of light **(John 15:19)**. We are defended and secured by heaven and watched over by the Supreme God. Knowing who you are and who you have been connected with will make you speak and act differently in the midst of chaos and challenges.

The Lord says, "Say ye not a confederacy to whom this people say a confederacy and fear not their fear." Are you speaking the same language with the world or is your language different? Can 10 men hold onto your skirt and say I want to follow you to your God? Is your confidence palpable? Can men run to you for a covering? Do you fear what they fear?

Brethren we are called to be different, we are called to speak differently, we are called to act differently, we are called to shine in darkness. When men are saying there is a casting down, we are to say there is a rising up **(Job 22:29)**. When men are saying, I am sick, inhabitants of Zion should not say I am sick (Isaiah 3:24). When men are saying, 'there is famine in the land' we should be saying, 'there is a hundred-fold harvest' **(Genesis 26:12)**. When men are saying there is darkness all over, we should say, we are lit up **(Isaiah 60:1-3)**. When men are saying, 'we are weak, we should say 'we are strong'. When they say, 'we are poor', we should be saying, 'we are rich' **(Joel 3:10)**. When men are saying, 'we cannot go up to fight the giants, we should say, 'let's go up at once and take the land' **(Numbers 13:30)**.

Our confidence in God is seen in our speeches and our actions in the midst of challenges. For we know that the counsel against us cannot stand, their association and proposals will be broken into pieces, for God is with us. Can your speech give you away like it did Peter in the midst of your colleagues? **(Matthew 26:73)**.

Choose to be different, choose to speak the language of the kingdom, choose to speak differently. Your words create your world. Cease from creating a chaotic world with your words, cease from releasing fear as you speak fear, stop to create famine as you declare famine, stop to multiply sickness as you speak sickness. You are a god that creates with words. Let's dare to say what God says even when you are antagonized and misunderstood. Speak positive words to see a positive world around you, speak peace to see a peaceful world, speak words of wisdom to attract men to Christ.

The good news is, no counsel of the wicked over our lives, and our world can stand, for God is with us. He will fix all things and bring to pass all that He told you. Rejoice the cloud that shows darkness to the world is the same that is shining light to the people of God. It's our season!

PRAYER: *Father, thank you for your word, stretch forth your hand and touch our tongue and heal it, help us master the language of heaven, let the world identify us by our words and actions in the midst of the prevailing darkness around us, in Jesus' name.*

Day 23

Fight Against Depression

Bible Reading: Psalms 42:11

"Why art thou cast down, O my soul? and why art thou disquieted within me? hope thou in God: for I shall yet praise him, who is the health of my countenance, and my God" **(Isaiah 8:12).**

Good morning, Family of the Faithful God, His loving-kindness is forever, hallelujah! Joy keeps your heavens open and gives you access to the wells of salvation **(Isaiah 12:3).** A joy-filled life is a God-filled life **(Romans 14:11).**

Brethren, depression is a weapon of the enemy to steal your joy and oppress you. The devil can easily oppress every depressed soul. An attack on your joy is an attack on your progress. Depression attacks your connection to your redemptive package, and your connection to the kingdom benefits. Depression locks your heaven; it causes delays to the promises of God **(1 Samuel 18-20)**; it attracts dryness and brings stagnation **(Joel 1:12).** Although David was a man after God's heart, he had seasons of depression in his life. He had challenges throughout his life and fought battles in the physical and spiritual but came out victorious.

How did David handle depression? How did he deal with discouragement?

He spent time speaking to his soul. He understood that man is a tripartite being. Man is a spirit with a soul and living in a body. He understood the weapon of soliloquizing (speaking to himself). He understood the weapon of meditation. He understood the weapon of thinking through in the face of challenges. Bible says and "David encouraged himself in the Lord **(1 Samuel 30:6)**. David also reasoned with his soul, saying, *"why are you cast down oh my soul...hope thou in the Lord..."* **(Psalms 42:5)**. He said, *"Bless the Lord Oh my soul and forget not all His benefits"* **(Psalms 103:1-3)**. He never waited for anyone to encourage him or for situations to change before giving God praise. He often found a reason to give God advance praise in the face of challenges. Is your soul cast down? Are you depressed because of the happenings around you, or are you anxious in your soul? Are you seeing others go forward, and it seems you are stagnated? Are you looking for a way through the challenges, and it seems farfetched? Is your countenance sad? Are you in a fix, imprisoned by circumstances around you? Are you looking back and full of regrets? Are you looking forward and can't see far? Is your future not set in your eyes?

Get up! Speak to your soul, encourage yourself in the Lord. David saw the challenges around him and knew it was another time for God to show himself faithful. He said, "Hope thou in the Lord for I will yet praise him for the help of his countenance" **(Psalms 42:11)**. See that challenge as another opportunity to praise the Lord! Challenges do not come to put you down but to raise you up. As the eagle is raised and propelled by the storms, so is the life of a child of God. Rejoice, therefore, for this one also has come to show God's faithfulness, loving-kindness, and strength. That challenge has come to bring out the best in you.

Orange juice cannot be produced if the orange is not squeezed. The oil in a palm fruit cannot be produced if it is not pounded and squeezed. The gold in the gold ore does not shine if it is not put in the fire. Naturally, the baby in the womb cannot be birthed if there is no squeezing through the birth canal. Get up! Give your soul instructions today, commune with your soul, remind him of the goodness of the Lord in your life in the past years and months, remind him of the victories you experienced in the last squeezing you had, and remind him of how God stepped in for you.

Your soul needs constant reminders and encouragement because the devil can easily deceive him. Your soul is unstable; circumstances can easily influence it. Get your spirit up; it has supremacy over your soul. Speak from your spirit to your soul. Did your spirit catch a glimpse of the victories God showed you as you appeared in his presence? Share your experience with your soul. Tell him what you heard in the place of prayer, the house of the Lord, or the word of God.

Arise this morning and say to your soul, "Rejoice, don't be cast down. We will yet praise God in this one also. Rejoice! Our sweetness and greatness are about to be birthed. The good news today is that "Yet the Lord will command his loving kindness in the daytime and His song shall be with you at night" You will break forth from the left and to the right. Joy will never cease from your habitation. It is not an end; it is a bend; this is not your end but a new level. God is too faithful to fail!

PRAYER: *Father, thank you for your word. Take away every depression from us, release the joy of the Lord into our spirit, give us your eyes to see the end from the beginning, open our eyes to see the way out, turn every challenge for our good and give us victory at the end, in the name of Jesus.*

Day 24

A New Word for a New Day

Bible Reading: 2 Samuel 5:19-25

"And David inquired of the Lord saying, shall I go up to the Philistine? Wilt thou deliver them into mine hand? And the Lord said unto David, Go up, for I will doubtless deliver the Philistines into thine hands" (2 Samuel 5:19).

Good morning, Family of the Faithful God, His mercy endures forever, hallelujah!

Brethren, the anointing of yesterday is not sufficient for today. The instructions for yesterday's issues might not be the same for today. The Lord gives direction per time. He instructs per time. David inquired of the Lord at first for instruction against the Philistines at Rephaim, and God said, *"Go up against, I will deliver them into thine hand."* The same enemies gathered again at the same place against the same king, but as David inquired, God said, *"Thou shalt not go up!"* God has various ways of dealing with your enemies. He is the all-wise God. His ways are past finding out; His wisdom is unfathomable.

Have you been promoted, elevated to your next level, or have you just overcome a challenge? Have you just been crowned a "king"? There are new devils at every new level because life is a battle. When the Philistines heard that David, who conquered and killed their warrior (Goliath), had been crowned king, they gathered against him. However, they were unaware that this king had a strategy that no one ever knew. A strategy that can never fail, a secret that keeps him victorious. He knew that "the battle is the Lord's".

What Was the Secret of David's Continuous Conquest?

He inquired of the Lord per time. David never depended on the instructions or the strategy of the last battle. He never went to battles without first getting instructions from the Commander and Captain of his life. David used fresh words to fight fresh battles. He had a "lion-ic" spirit in him. Lions never eat stale meat for sustenance but feed on fresh blood. There is a fresh word for a fresh day. There is a fresh instruction per battle. There is a fresh directive for each new level. Are you going into your new battle with an old instruction? Did God say "Go up" at first, and you are going again with the same instruction of yesterday? Though the situation might be the same, the enemy the same, the location the same, the day is different, and the time is different. Jesus said, sufficient is the day's trouble.

Brethren, going to battle without the backing of the one who fights for you is equivalent to being defeated in the battle. You don't have the might of your own. It is not by power, might, wisdom, experience, or expertise that one wins battles in life, but by the Spirit of God, the unseen hand that can turn a pebble into a weapon of destruction **(1 Samuel 17)**. The Spirit of God turns a jaw bone into a weapon of war **(Judges 15:15)** and turns praise into a weapon of mass destruction **(2 Chronicles 20:20-22)**. Moses said, "If your presence does not go with us, take us not up". Do you depend on your strength?

The Bible says, *"Trust in the Lord with all your heart and lean not unto your understanding, in all your ways acknowledge him and he shall direct thy path"* **(Proverbs 3:5-6)**. It's time to stop fighting your battles with old instructions. It's time to go down to your stronghold and inquire of the Lord for a fresh word. It's time to stop working on the instruction God gave to your father; it's time to get your own word' You are lion-ic in nature, a descendant of the Lion of the tribe of Judah. Go then for "fresh blood" every day.

Every day opens to a new battle, a new challenge that needs a solution. Ask this per time "Dear Lord, which way should I go, what do I do? How, where, when and what?" The good news is that victory is ahead of you today. A solution to your challenge is nigh unto you even in your mouth. The 'Goliath' in your life is defeated; the "Philistines" coming against you at your new level are all defeated. Congratulations on your victories!

PRAYER: *Father, thank you for your faithfulness. We come before you to inquire of you. We come to you for directives on what to do. Show us how and when to go after what we seek and where to find help. Lead us, oh Lord, to the place of victory, in Jesus' mighty name.*

Day 25

Your Honor, Their Shame

Bible Reading: Esther 6:10

"Then the king said to Haman, "Hurry, take the robe and the horse, as you have suggested, and do so for Mordecai the Jew who sits within the king's gate! Leave nothing undone of all that you have spoken."" **(Esther 6:10).**

Good morning, Family of The Rewarder-God, He is full of wonders, hallelujah!

Brethren, God works in mysterious ways. The eyes of the Lord run to-and-fro throughout the whole earth, to shew himself strong on behalf of those whose heart is perfect toward him **(2 Chronicles 16:9)**. *Why then do the heathen rage and the people imagine a vain thing, the kings of the earth take counsel against the Lord and against his anointed ones* **(Psalms 2:1-2)**. Why then do the people of God fear their enemies' rumblings, noise, and plans? Do they not know, have they not heard that the everlasting God, the Lord, the Creator of the ends of the earth, fainted not, neither is weary? **(Isaiah 40:28-31)**. Do they not know that it is He who fights for

His children? Do they not see He is the same yesterday, today and forever? What He does for one, He does for all?

Sleep was taken away from the king Ahasuerus because wicked Haman was awake planning evil for Mordecai. God overtook Him, arrived at the king's palace, and overturned things before his arrival. His sleepless night was in futility. No one can kick against the pricks and remain unhurt. Haman's plans were silenced and never saw the light of the day. God turned his evil plans to his shame.

Haman went home in disgrace, while Mordecai went home honoured. The same mouth he had prepared to put Mordecai to a shameful death is the same mouth he used to pronounce his honour **(Esther 6)**. Balak hired Balaam to curse the Israelites, but he began to bless them instead, for the Lord had turned things around. It is impossible to curse whom the Lord has blessed. Fear not, dear child of God, fear not their plans against your destiny, fear not what the world fears. Your Father controls the heart of the king. The whole world is in His hands, working everything for your good.

Their counsel He will turn to foolishness, their gallows they will hang in it, their flesh and blood, they'll eat and drink by themselves, their sword they will use to destroy one another. The time of maturity and execution of the evil plan against you is the time of your elevation and promotions by God. They have shut you down, but it is your time of explosion and multiplication. It is a time of your beautification. God is turning things around in your favour. Your delay is not denial; your delayed reward is waiting for time; your delayed answer to your prayers is waiting for the cup of your enemies to be full.

Double honour awaits you in the season. Your detractors shall be the same to decorate you. As Haman arrayed and announced the promotion of Mordecai, so shall your enemies announce you to their shame. Fear not. God is fighting your battles; God is fixing up your helper; God is exchanging things; God is turning and transferring things in this lockdown. We are emerging more than conquerors. The night of the death cry in Egypt was also the night of liberation and exodus of the Israelites. Fear not; God is not asleep. He sees all things, knows all things. He works day and night to bring you to your place of honour.

PRAYER: *Thank you, Father, for your word. We surrender all to you. Have your way, Lord. We are waiting on you. We wait on you to destroy every Haman around our life and destiny. Let anyone that digs a pit for us fall into it, bring shame and reproach to them that plan shame for us in Jesus' name.*

Day 26

Wait for Divine Timing

Bible Reading: John 2:4

"Woman, why involve me?" Jesus replied. "My hour has not yet come" **(John 2:4).**

Good morning, Family of the On-time God. Awesome are You, Lord! Brethren, there is a season for everything, and there is a time for every purpose under the earth **(Ecclesiastes 3:1).**

Many have lived in fear and anxiety because they fail to understand the timing of God. Many have lost trust in God and made God look like the wicked judge **(Luke 18:1-5).** They have failed to realize that the sun and the moon were created for times and seasons for the inhabitants of the earth **(Genesis 1:14-15).**

Some have failed to realize that we live in different time zones in God's agenda. Some have prayed for years and cried uncontrollably and hopelessly because they see the sun shine in another's time zone and expect their sun to shine also on them. You can't wake someone in America from

Nigeria by 6 am Nigerian time to go to work. His time zone is different from that in Nigeria.

There is a time slated for everything. The gestation period for a dog is 3 months, a goat is 5 months, a cat is 67 days, a chicken is 21 days, an elephant is 1 and a half years, and man is 9 months. Can a woman who is 3 months pregnant, seeing her neighbor, friend, sister, or colleague deliver her baby at 9 months, begin crying for her baby to come forth the same day also? Can we pray for an unripe mango fruit to ripen the same day? Can we cry and pray, asking God to bring the morning at 10 pm?

Brethren, there is a time for everything. Morning comes on its own accord when the night is over; the baby comes when the expected date of delivery arrives; the fruit ripens when its time is due. Why then do men cry and wallow in pain and anxiety? Some have brought forth prematurely when their blessings were not matured. Some have brought forth trouble because they asked for a permissive will of God to be done.

Moses was the deliverer sent by God to deliver the Israelites from bondage after 400 years, but he jumped the gun prematurely. He had to be taken to the wilderness in Midian to be trained on how to wait. Abraham and Sarah decided to help God fulfill His promise prematurely, and Ishmael, the one enemy of Israel, was born. Are you anxious, thinking that God does not care or is too slow to His word, or is partial?

Your timing is different from your neighbor's timing. Your time also may not be God's time. Delay is not denial; He cannot break His covenant with you. He is true to His word and can never lie. There is no turning of shadow with Him. Terah had a delay, but Abraham was still born when he was 70 years old; Abraham had a delay, but Isaac still came at 100 years; Esau and Jacob still came after Isaac's delay (20 years); Joseph was still born after Rachel's delay.

You might call it delay, but God calls it due time. The elephant and chicken, having conceived the same day, do not mean they will give birth the same day. Some of us are pregnant with an elephant - kind of dream, for a special 'baby,' business, job, marriage, ministry. We should not expect our deliveries to be in 21 days. Jesus says, "My hour is not yet come." Let the old wine be totally exhausted before He brings the new.

Moses was emptied out in the wilderness, the pride as a prince of Egypt, his impatience, Egyptian nature emptied out in the wilderness. He became the meekest man that ever lived. He was matured after 40 years of training to wait and lead the sheep of God for 40 years. Some of us are in that wilderness being trained; some are carrying 'an elephant'; some are bringing forth deliverers. Though it tarries, wait for it; it shall surely come; it shall not tarry **(Habakkuk 2:3)**.

Be anxious for nothing **(Philippians 4:6)**, for He makes all things beautiful in His time **(Ecclesiastes 3:11)**. As long as the covenant of day and night is in place, His covenant with you cannot be broken **(Jeremiah 33:20)**. Wait on the Lord and be of good courage, and the Lord will strengthen your heart **(Psalms 27:14)**. You shall be like a tree planted by rivers of water that brings forth its fruit in its season **(Psalms 1:3)**. The good news is, your Expected Date of Delivery is here and is peculiar to you. God is visiting someone this week; someone's story is turning around.

PRAYER: *Father, thank you for your word. We patiently wait on you. Forgive us if we have prayed and cried for premature deliveries, if we have questioned your faithfulness in our actions. Forgive our anxiety and frustrations. We trust you to bring our blessings to pass at your perfect timing. In Jesus' name, we pray. Amen.*

Day 27

Forget Not His Benefits

Bible Reading: Psalms 103:2

"Bless the Lord, O my soul, and forget not all his benefits" **(Psalms 103:2).**

Good morning, Family of the Almighty God! He is mighty in all His ways —hallelujah!

Brethren, we tend to forget the greatness of our God when we face great challenges. The magnitude of our challenges clouds our reasoning, and we tend to forget the mighty hand of God that delivered us from enemies who were too strong for us. We forget that our victories in previous battles were not by our own power but by the invisible hand of God.

David often remembered the mighty hand of God that granted him victories. His faith was always boosted to face his challenges with boldness. He recalled his deliverance from the lion and the bear, and Goliath became as nothing before him **(1 Samuel 17:34-36).**

What are the benefits of remembering the mighty acts of God?

1. It boosts your faith in God.
2. It connects you to the power source.
3. It magnifies the Lord in your spirit above your challenges.
4. It belittles your challenges.
5. It invites God to inhabit your praises and work victory over every negative circumstance in your life.

Are you facing a challenge that seems greater than you can handle? Forget not His benefits. Go back and review God's track record. Remember who is in the battle with you, who fought and is fighting for you. Remember that He is the Almighty God—your Healer, Provider, Sustainer, Nourisher, Lifter-upon-your-head, Strength, and Helper, among other things.

Forget not His benefits; He heals all diseases, forgives all iniquities, redeems your life from destruction, satisfies your mouth with good things, and crowns you with loving-kindness and tender mercies. The God who saw you through those years, months, weeks, and days of pain, fears, and sickness is not weary or weaker today. He is the same yesterday, today, and forever. What He did yesterday, He can and will do for you today. Fear not! Begin to count your benefits, and He will come through for you in this situation as well.

The good news is, He never leaves you nor forsakes you. When you pass through the waters, He will be with you; when you go through the fire, it will not burn you **(Isaiah 43:2)**. Even in the valley of the shadow of death, He is with you **(Psalms 23:4)**. Cheer up! Your Master and Lord are on duty, and He never fails.

PRAYER: *Thank you, Jesus, for your faithfulness. Bestow upon us the garment of praise that we may remember your benefits and glorify your name. Overcome every pressing need, impossible challenge, and every flood that has come against us. Make us more than conquerors in Jesus' name. Amen.*

Day 28

Your Pride, Your Strength

Bible Reading: Daniel 2:17-19

"Then Daniel went in to his house and made the thing known to Hananiah, Mishael, and Azariah, his companions...Then the secret was revealed unto Daniel by night" (Daniel 2:17,19).

Good morning, Family of the God of Hosts! His mercy endures forever, and His love is renewed every morning—hallelujah!

Brethren, God made the solitary into families **(Psalm 68:6)**. He is the God of hosts **(Zechariah 4:6)**. While God is God by Himself, He operates with His hosts. Lions most often walk together; they belong to a social family called a pride and form a formidable team against any attack. One can chase a thousand, and two can put ten thousand to flight **(Deuteronomy 32:20)**. We have a lion-like nature and belong to the family of the Lion of the tribe of Judah. Therefore, we are to exhibit His character and likeness.

Daniel and his friends were about to be attacked and killed at the king's instruction, but he retreated to his pride of lions who stood by him to seek God's face, and the answer came. They were all delivered from death **(Daniel 2:17-19)**.

Peter also had his pride. He was arrested and imprisoned to be killed, but his pride gathered and roared against the evil king's plan, and his deliverance came **(Acts 12:3-19)**.

Jesus, the Son of God, had His pride of twelve disciples. He went about with His pride, occasionally retreated to quiet places to pray, and returned to His pride. In the time of His impending death, He took the disciples to stand with Him in prayer, and God's will for His life was established **(Matthew 26:37-46)**.

If you are a "lion," do you have a "pride"?

What is a pride?

A pride is a group of lions, typically numbering 15-30 lions. Years ago, I watched a documentary where a solitary lion was harassed by a group of hyenas because he was alone. There was no help for him because he was alone. His life was nearly taken until members of his pride arrived and dealt with the hyenas.

Are you thinking you are strong? Are you a lonely lion roaring alone in the forest? While social distancing may be the order of the day today, spiritual distancing is even more dangerous. The devil roams the earth, seeking out lonely Christians—those who think they can make it on their own, those who believe they can fight battles alone. It's time to wake up! Get back to your pride, attach yourself to a pride, and connect with your pride. Send signals to your pride to synergize against every enemy. No wild animal can harass a pride of lions, but they can harass and weary a lonely lion.

Arise and connect with your pride this morning. Have you prayed alone for a long time concerning an attack from the enemy with no answers in view? The answer is waiting for synergy. One can chase a thousand, but two can put ten thousand to flight **(Deuteronomy 32:20)**. Two are better than one, for if one falls, the other will raise him up **(Ecclesiastes 4:9-10)**. Whether you are a Pastor or a child of God, get a pride to walk with. Go back to your pride and strengthen your bond. A threefold cord cannot easily be broken. Return to your pride, return to your source of energy, return to the place where God blesses you **(Psalms 133:1-3)**.

The good news is that God is with you as a mighty, terrible one. He will not allow the enemy to exact upon you, nor will the son of wickedness afflict you **(Psalms 89:22)**.

PRAYER: *Father, we thank you for your word. Help us return to the fellowship of our brethren, that we may dwell together in unity and stand together to defeat the enemies of our souls and destinies. In Jesus' name, we pray. Amen.*

Day 29

Faith: The Speaking Force

Bible Reading: Mark 4:39

"Then He arose and rebuked the wind, and said to the sea, 'Peace, be still!' And the wind ceased and there was a great calm" **(Mark 4:39).**

Good morning, Family of the Living God! Great is His faithfulness —hallelujah!

Brethren, the journey of life is full of storms, even when the call comes from the King of kings. The presence of the King of kings in our lives does not exclude storms, fire, mountains, and challenges. It actually attracts more of them. However, the good news is that every victory builds up our faith and makes us giants in the kingdom. Every storm strengthens the muscle of our faith and draws us closer to our God. Storms open our eyes to see the greatness of His power **(Mark 4:41).**

Jesus said to His disciples, "Let us go over to the other side," and He entered the boat to begin the journey with them. However, a fierce storm raged upon the boat, even with Jesus, the Master, on board. Why did the waves fill up the boat when Jesus, the Master of the Universe and the Head of all principalities and powers, was in the boat with them? Why did He seem to be asleep, as if He did not care? The disciples struggled on their own, dealing with the waves, doing everything they could to stop the water from entering the boat. They did nothing to address the storm, the source of their challenges. The waves kept pouring in until the boat was full.

Sometimes, Jesus seems to be asleep when we are in our storms. He appears distant and uncaring, but hold on—He is in the boat with you! Where was the faith of the disciples? They had witnessed the mighty works that Jesus had done, they had seen the sick healed, and great miracles were wrought by His hands. Why did Jesus label them as fearful with no faith? Sometimes, we become so accustomed to seeing miracles that we take them for granted, and we believe we can handle certain problems with our own strength.

Until we turn to Him in faith, storms will not cease. Why don't we speak words of faith to the storms and calm them? Faith is a speaking force. It's because there are no abundant words of God in our hearts to speak out. "For with the heart one believes unto righteousness, and with the mouth confession is made unto salvation" **(Romans 10:10-11)**. Your faith can be seen by the words you speak in the face of challenges. It can also be seen through your actions and the confidence you exhibit in the midst of storms.

Storms come to elevate and strengthen your faith in God; their purpose is not to drown you. Do not fear, for the Master of the sea is in your boat. Although it may seem He is sleeping, call on Him, and He will rebuke that storm. Jesus expected the disciples to deal with the storm by speaking to it, but their lack of faith hindered them. There was nothing inside them to speak out. Feed your faith with the word of God to store up faith for use in times of challenges.

Fear not, for He who began a good work in you will bring it to an expected end. He who called you will also do it. He is the Alpha and Omega, the Beginning and the End, the First and the Last. His boat can never sink halfway through the journey. You will surely arrive at the shore rejoicing.

PRAYER: *Father, we thank you for your word. Help us, O Lord, to increase our faith daily. We will not lose faith in the face of our challenges. Bring our storms to an end. We speak peace to our lives, minds, homes, businesses, ministries, marriages, children, and more, in Jesus' mighty name. Amen.*

Day 30

Fear Not!

Bible Reading: Isaiah 43:2

"When you pass through the waters, I will be with you; and when you pass through the rivers, they will not sweep over you. When you walk through the fire, you will not be burned; the flames will not set you ablaze" **(Isaiah 43:2).**

Good morning, Family of the Savior and Redeemer, faithful are You, O Lord.

Brethren, fear is an enemy of faith, and fear has torment. Fear to a child of God is false evidence appearing real. The spirit of fear is a weapon of the enemy; it is an advance team that precedes all attacks of the enemy. Fear cripples a child of God and causes them to lose faith in their Savior and Redeemer. Fear belittles God and His power in the heart of a child of God.

Fear has torments because it creates vivid pictures in the mind of a believer and controls the actions of anyone it is sent to. Defeating this devil's advance team is defeating the enemy. When one succumbs to its tricks and wiles, they succumb to the power of the enemy, and they become oppressed and depressed.

How do you fight fear? Meditate on the power of God and His mighty works. Search out His marvelous works that He did in the past. Hear Him daily. Troubles and challenges are part of life. The Bible says, "when" and not "if" you pass through the waters, rivers, and fires. Don't be taken by surprise and lose faith when challenges come. Seek your Savior who assures you of salvation, refuge, and His presence. God can never lie; nothing takes Him by surprise. He knows the end from the beginning. He saw when they gathered to afflict; He knew what they planned, He waited for them to gather, and He knows what to do to scatter them. He is not too late for you.

He allowed Pharaoh to chase after the children of Israel because He had a plan to drown them all in the sea. Fear not, God has the plan in His hands; He has you in the hollow of His hands; you are precious in His sight. He cannot leave you nor forsake you. Trust in the Lord with all your heart. Lean not onto what your little mind can comprehend. His thoughts are not your thoughts, neither your ways His ways. Fear not, He called you out of Egypt to bring you to the promised land; the sea, Pharaoh, the wilderness, the serpent bite, and the Jordan notwithstanding. He is able, more than able. He is able more than able to accomplish all that concerns you today. He can and will deliver you out of every fire, waters, or rivers.

Get up! Stand up, out of that dust, and get to the house of the Lord, where you will be given understanding of the happenings and what the will of God is concerning your life.

PRAYER: *Father, thank you for your word. Help us to depend on, trust in, and believe in you and your word. Help our unbelief and strengthen us on the inside. We trust you to settle us after we have suffered a while. Thank you, Lord, in Jesus' name.*

Day 31

God Of All Possibilities

Bible Reading: Exodus 14:13-14

"Fear not, stand still, and see the salvation of the Lord, which He will show you today, for the Egyptians whom you see today, you shall see them no more forever. The LORD will fight for you and you shall hold your peace" **(Exodus 14:13-14).**

Good morning, Family of the God of all possibilities, His mercy endures forever—hallelujah!

Brethren, God is a God of war; He specializes in battles. Battles are tests that take you to your next level. The children of Israel, excited that they had finally left the place of bondage, must have been praising God for His mighty acts in Egypt. But suddenly, they looked, and their enemies were chasing hard after them. They cried unto the Lord. The Lord heard the cry of Moses and came to their rescue. God is a God of all possibilities; there is nothing He cannot do, nothing He cannot change, and nothing He cannot turn around.

The enemies did not stop pursuing them because God had a plan. God did not send the enemy back the way they came but caused them to press forward into the Red Sea, where they were drowned. He did the impossible, made a way through the sea, and His children crossed over to the other side.

Are you in a fretful moment? Are you trying to figure out what to do in your battlefield? Fear not, all He is asking you to do is to go forward; keep believing, keep trusting, keep seeing the future He promised you. Don't look back; don't wish to turn back. God is fighting for you. It might not seem so. The presence of God (the Cloud) that had been leading you might not be there anymore. The Cloud moved from in front of them and went behind them. Fear not, He did not leave you; He went behind to fight. He can do the impossible, He can do what has never happened in the history of humanity just for you, because He loves you.

The good news this morning is that the Egyptians you see today, you will see them no more. Fear not, stand still, and see the salvation of the Lord.

PRAYER: *Father, we thank you for being there when we call. Thank you for your word today. Give us peace in our storm; give us full understanding of your presence in our fire. Deliver us speedily out of the fire as you did for Shadrach, Meshach, and Abednego. We give you thanks for speedy answers, in Jesus' name.*

Day 32

The Fourth Man in Your Fire

Bible Reading: Daniel 3:25

"He answered and said, 'Lo, I see four men loose, walking in the midst of the fire, and they have no hurt; and the form of the fourth is like the Son of God'" (Daniel 3:25).

Good morning, Family of the Wonder-Working God; He is mighty to save —hallelujah!

Brethren, God is a covenant-keeping God; He is the Almighty. There is absolutely nothing too hard for Him to do. He can suspend natural occurrences, bring heaven's atmosphere to earth, make time go back, make a way through the water, turn night into day and day into night, turn fire into a cool environment to walk in. He can walk upon the waters of your life, raise a standard against the floods of your life, make your ark float on the flood that is drowning others, raise the dead back to life, heal the blind, open prison doors of their own accord, use an earthquake to open prison doors, shut the mouths of lions, kill your "Goliath" with a stone, rain fire and brimstone, restore lost glory in a moment, make an old woman a mother of children, make your "axe head" float in water, bring water out of the rock, feed 3 million people without money for 40 years. He is a Sovereign God.

I'm introducing the Fourth Man in the fire; Jesus, the Son of God, who is and was and is to come. He is the same yesterday, today, and forever. He was in the beginning; all things were made by Him, and there was nothing that was made that was not made by Him (John 1). He has the capacity to make, to create anything that He wishes to create and recreate. Nothing moves Him (Psalms 46). The Fourth Man says, "I will never leave you nor forsake you", "I will be with you in trouble", "I will help you", "when you pass through the fire it will not burn you, and through the waters it will not overflow you". He says, "I will not leave you nor forsake you", "I am with you always even unto the end of the age". He went about doing good and healing all them that were oppressed by the devil (Acts 10:38). He says, "my meat is to do the will of God and finish it". He was sent as the Savior. He is still saving men out of their distresses because He is alive and lives forever.

Is there any fire that you have been put in? Has the fire been increased 7 times by the wicked? Have they tied every part of you and thrown you into the fire? The good news is, the Fourth Man is at the scene; He has been there from the beginning. He had gone into the fire to wait for you. Why did He not avert the fire? Why did He not stop the people from setting up the fire? Did He come late when they had thrown them into the fire? Never! God never comes late to any situation; He comes earlier than the devil, earlier than you. Do you prepare the place for His glory to be revealed?

Shadrach, Meshach, and Abednego, bound and thrown into the fire, were loosed and walking in the fire; that is wonder personified. You sometimes need to be in a fire to gain the title "A sign and a wonder". How then will men run to you if the same events and results that happen to common men happen to you? Your case is different; your situation is different; what affects others is not permitted to happen to you because you are a "Show-piece of the Almighty God". He wants to show the world what He can do; He has chosen you to make His power known to the world and to silence the devil forever. Wait, be still, and see the salvation that He will bring to you. As the three Hebrew boys emerged from the fire loosed, and men marveled at them, seeing that the fire had no power over their body, their hair singed not, their coats did not change, the smell of fire was not on them. So shall you be a marvel to your world. Be rest assured that the Fourth Man; The Son of God, is in that fire, and it will surely, without fail, turn to a testimony for you. Say, "The Son of God is in the fire with me; I am coming out unscathed to the glory of God".

PRAYER: *Father, thank you for your faithfulness, thank you for your word today. Give us peace in our storm, give us full understanding of your presence in our fire. Deliver us speedily out of the fire as you did Shadrach, Meshach, and Abednego. We give you thanks for speedy answers, in Jesus' name.*

Day 33

The Author and Finisher

Bible Reading: Zechariah 4:1-9

"The hands of Zerubbabel have laid the foundation of this house; his hands shall also finish it; and thou shalt know that the LORD of hosts hath sent me unto you" (Zechariah 4:9).

Brethren, our God is the Beginning, and He is the End, the First and the Last, the Author and Finisher, Alpha and Omega. He cannot be stopped or harassed by any devil. He controls the affairs of all men. He is the Head of all principalities and powers **(Colossians 2:10)**. His wisdom is unfathomable. Has He started with you in any project? Has He given you a word at the beginning? Have storms of life met you on your way to where God said He was taking you to? He has sent His word to you this today, "It's not by might, nor power but by His Spirit". The arm of flesh might fail you but the One that sent you forth at the beginning is able to take you across the sea. He is able to calm the storm that has ensued in the midst of the year.

Jesus said to the disciples "Let us go over to the other side" He speaks in His capacity and not yours. It is not by your strength that you will make it there; it is by His Spirit and by His grace. Whatever He says, He creates, nothing can stop it. As the storm could not stop the disciples from going over to the other side, they arrived at the shore. Surely, you cannot be stopped **(Luke 8:22-26)**.

As the storms, trials, and temptations did not stop the Israelites from getting into Canaan, no circumstance can stop you. You can only be delayed but not denied. Your delay is to fit into God's timing for your life. Joseph waited in the pit, Potiphar's house, and prison until his appointed time to be enthroned came. The enemy meant it for evil but God is turning it around to work together for your good.

Get up! Fear not! Cheer up and give the Alpha and Omega the praise. He is faithful, He cannot lie, He is dependable.

PRAYER: *Father, thank you because your word is yea and amen. Speak to our mountains to be brought low. We trust you who began the good work, who also will complete it in us, in Jesus' name.*

Day 34

God of David Is Unchangeable

Bible Reading: 2 Samuel 21:1-22

"And there was yet a battle in Gath, where was a man of great stature, that had on every hand six fingers, and on every foot six toes, four and twenty in number; and he also was born to the giant" **(2 Samuel 21:20).**

Good morning, Family of the God of war; He is Mighty in battle, Almighty is He—hallelujah!

Brethren, there is a perpetual battle because there is a devil who continuously antagonizes the plan of God for His children. He is ever envious of our position in God where he lost because of pride and has therefore vowed never to let peace be with God's children. The good news is that there is a predestined victory kept for all who trust in Him; there is victory already pre-determined by our Father. It is already settled in heaven and cannot be changed **(Psalm 119:89).** Jesus on the cross sealed the deal **(John 19:30, John 19:22).**

David killed the giant of Gath named Goliath, and there was so much jubilation, songs of praise began to flood the air in Israel, and God's name was glorified as He defeated their enemies. However, there was another battle with Isbi-benob; another giant came out after him, and Israel, but God delivered Israel from this giant. And again, another battle with Saph; another giant, and David's men slew him. Again, another battle with the brother of Goliath whom David slew, and again Israel defeated him and got them victory. And yet another battle in Gath, and a similitude of Goliath emerged again to fight the children of Israel, but Jonathan, the brother of David, slew him also.

Does this sound like your life? Are you facing battle after battle that looks unending? Are you going from one challenge to another; it seems you are getting weary? The Bible says "and David went down, and his servants with him, and fought against the Philistines, and David waxed faint" **(2 Samuel 21:15)**. David waxed faint, but His God who fights for him never grows weary nor faints. He can raise men to fight for you. The God that killed Goliath by the hand of David raised men to fight, and the 4 giants were discomfited, even with David's absence in the battlefield **(2 Samuel 21:17)**.

Don't give up; you are not alone; the battle over your life and destiny is not yours; it is the Lord's. Cheer up! Those who are for you are more than those that are fighting against you. The Lord has raised helpers for you already. Those giants that have risen up against you will be defeated also. The God of David and the armies of Israel is unchangeable; He is too faithful to fail. He is dependable. The victory is already won. The giants of Gath came up with different names to kill and destroy, but they all went down defeated. Cheer up; the same devil that was defeated last time is the same that has risen against you this time wearing another face and bearing another name. He is no big deal for your God who defeated him last time.

Note: We are not fighting against flesh and blood but against the devil's demonic hierarchy. However, the head of all principalities is the one fighting for you, and you are seated with him in heavenly places far above the highest hierarchy of the devil. Victory is sure! Victory is sure!! Victory is sure!!! It is impossible for God to fail! You may be weary, but your 'Abishai,' 'Sibbechal,' 'Elhanan,' and 'Jonathan' have been released to slay your giants and bring them completely down. You belong to Him, and God is fighting for you whether you wax faint or not. Another victory song is ringing again; I can hear the sound of Victory, hallelujah!

PRAYER: *Father, there is no one like you, great in battle; Jehovah is your name. Thank you for your faithfulness; thank you for the release of my helpers to me. Thank you because the giant before me had already been defeated; thank you because of the victory song you have given to us this morning. Bring these giants down speedily, like you have always done. Thank you, the Great I am that I am; you are too faithful to fail; you are dependable. Praise awaits you in Zion, in Jesus' name.*

Day 35

Forgiveness and Unforgiveness

Bible Reading: Luke 11:1-4

"And forgive us our sins, for we ourselves also forgive everyone who is indebted to us [who has offended us or done us wrong]" **(Luke 11:4) AMP.**

Good morning, most wonderful family of the merciful God. Unforgiveness and being unforgiven is one of the most dangerous and cancerous vices in the life of a human being, even in Christendom today. Unforgiveness, regrettably, is an offshoot of lawlessness! And most of the time, we discover that what causes or brings about this vice is something that could easily have been ignored or overlooked if we had been a little more patient.

Granted, there are things which can really provoke one to anger, but now ask yourself, is it enough reason for me to risk losing my life and soul eternally? Oh yes, it can be quite difficult to forget and forgive, especially in cases of murder, defamation of character, abduction, and others! But then, we often and always pray, yet, deeply seated in our hearts is bitterness, anger, and unforgiveness toward some people who have offended us in one way or another.

Interestingly, there are also people that hold others in unforgiveness without the people even knowing! And they pretend before these people when they see them. That's pure hypocrisy! In Ephesians 4:31-32, the Bible says, "Let all bitterness and indignation and wrath (passion, rage, bad temper) and resentment (anger, animosity) and quarreling (brawling, clamor, contention) and slander (evil-speaking, abusive or blasphemous language) be banished from you, with all malice (spite, ill will, or baseness of any kind). And become useful and helpful and kind to one another, tenderhearted (compassionate, understanding, loving-hearted), forgiving one another [readily and freely], as God in Christ forgave you" (AMP).

God had determined to forgive us even before we sinned. It's a decision He had taken, even though with a small clause added, that "If we [freely] admit that we have sinned and confess our sins, He is faithful and just (true to His own nature and promises) and will forgive our sins [dismiss our lawlessness] and [continuously] cleanse us from all unrighteousness [everything not in conformity to His will in purpose, thought, and action]" **(1 John 1:9, AMP)**.

PRAYER: *Father, in the name of Jesus, in your mercy, I plead for forgiveness over any of my trespasses. I denounce any spirit of unforgiveness from this day henceforth, in Jesus' name.*

Day 36

Jesus Is Risen

Bible Reading: Matthew 28:1-7

"He is not here; He is risen, as he said. Come, see the place where the Lord lay." (Matthew 28:6).

Hallelujah! Jesus is risen. Glory to God. Family, I'm so glad this morning that we are celebrating our risen Christ. Buddha has a birth date, Mohammed has a birth date, Guru Maharaji has a birth date, Olumba Obu has a birth date, and Our Lord Jesus also has a birth date. But what distinguishes all of them from Our King is that none of these has a RESURRECTION day except our Lord Jesus. Hallelujah!

The stone was rolled away, and He is risen. He did not rise alone, but the Bible says we died with Him, and we are also raised with Him. What could not hold HIM down cannot hold you down. The forces that could not stop HIM from coming out of the grave cannot stop you either. The lies that the guards told about HIS resurrection have not cancelled the truth that He is risen. The lies that the circumstance is telling concerning your life cannot change the fact that you are risen.

Let's shout for joy today that He is risen, and we are risen with Him also. Let joy spring forth from the inside and celebrate Jesus today, celebrate the end of all wickedness in your life, celebrate that the stone that caged you in has been rolled away and sat upon. Thank you, Jesus!

PRAYER: *Father, thank you for your word. Let our graves be opened; let us come out of what caged us in. Breathe your life into us, in Jesus' name.*

Day 37

Judge Not

Bible Reading: Mattthew 7:1-3

"Judge not, that ye be not judged" **(Matthew 7:1).**

Good morning, the wonderful family of the God of mercy and love. We are alive again today, Hallelujah! We praise you, our Father, forever. Brethren, God's word is a lamp that lights all darkness in our lives.

Have you been caught in a web of judging others? Have you seen others as not righteous or dedicated to their service to God as you are? Have you fallen into the temptation of complaining about what others are doing or not doing? His word has come this morning, Judge not that you will not be judged **(Matthew 7:1).**

Our position and dedication are not of our own making; the grace to do service is of God. It is by election of grace that we are what we are, where we are, and accomplished all we have. Let's not hold ourselves higher than others and look down on others who have not attained our heights in Christ **(1 Timothy 1:9).**

The Bible says, "let he that stands take heed lest he falls" **(1 Corinthians 10:12)**. It is not of him that willeth or of him that runneth but of God that showeth mercy **(Romans 9:16)**. If there was no Judas among the disciples, the Son of God would not have been sold and crucified; if there was no Pharaoh, there would not have been the bondage which led to the show of God's mighty hands in Egypt.

The word of God makes us understand that your salvation is not of works; any should boast. Our works will only show off our righteousness, which is as filthy rags before God. Every one of our brethren brought into our lives, whether "good" or "bad," is for our good, to help in the building of lives. Let's love all that are in the kingdom, judge not and pray for all, even those who persecute or despise us. For in this will they know that we are the Children of God. If all were righteous, we won't have souls to win for Christ; if all were good, we won't be aware of the fruits of the spirit we bear. The brightness of the stars can only be seen in the night. I pray this morning that we will begin to see the good in every one of our brethren and pray for them who are going against the law of our God.

PRAYER: *Father, we pray that you give us your eyes to see as you see, your mind to reason as you do, and your Spirit to love as you love, in Jesus' mighty name.*

Day 38

Make Use of Your Mouth

Bible Reading: Genesis 1:1-31

"And God said, Let there be light: and there was light" **(Genesis 1:3).**

Good morning, Family of the Omnipresent God. It's the day that the LORD has made; we shall rejoice and be glad in it. We shall doubtlessly return, bringing our sheaves with us, hallelujah!

Sometimes it seems help is very far away, and you do not know who to run to. Your answer is in your mouth; the Word of deliverance, hope, healing, protection, breakthrough is in your tongue **(Romans 10:4)**. God, in Genesis 1, had a chaotic situation; He began to speak to the formless and void world and had it as He wanted. Brethren, that desire is in your mouth. Begin to call those things that be not as if they were **(Hebrews 11:3)**. Believe in your heart that those things which you desire will come to pass; then make declarations concerning your desires. Fear not; speak them into being. Your victory is already won.

Day 39

Your Miracle Has Finally Come

Bible Reading: Mark 6:1-6

"And when the sabbath day was come, he began to teach in the synagogue: and many hearing him were astonished, saying, From whence hath this man these things? and what wisdom is this which is given unto him, that even such mighty works are wrought by his hands?" **(Mark 6:2).**

Good morning, family of the miracle-working God. Great is His faithfulness; morning by morning new mercies we see, hallelujah!

Jesus, the miracle worker ,went to His own country and could do no mighty works there **(Mark 6:5)**. What a calamity? Why this? Unbelief and familiarity with the vessel used! This has robbed many believers of their long-awaited breakthrough, healings, deliverances, and inheritance in Christ.

The vessel you disregard cannot be a blessing to you. Jesus' people knew Him as Mary's son, the carpenter, and could not draw virtues from Him to deal with their troubles. Brethren, let's watch out and be spiritually sensitive; God can use anyone this season to give you the connection you need, to bring you to your next level. Let's not call common whom God has anointed **(Acts 10:13-15)**. Your house help **(2 Kings 5:2-3)**, guard **(1 Samuel 9:7-8)**, gateman **(Esther 6)**, brother, sister, friend can be the anointed one. The Pastor that you are too familiar with can be the one carrying that blessing this season. Let's value everyone around us in this season of divine connectivity.

PRAYER: *I pray that as God sends these angels to us to take us to our next level, we will recognize them as Abraham did, and Isaac came. I pray for God to give us His eyes and mind, so we will not miss our angel, in Jesus' name. Remember it's our week of divine connectivity. Congratulations in advance!*

Day 40

You Will Get There

Bible Reading: Esther 2:1-17

"And he brought up Hadassah, that is, Esther, his uncle's daughter: for she had neither father nor mother, and the maid was fair and beautiful; whom Mordecai, when her father and mother were dead, took for his own daughter" **(Esther 2:7).**

Good morning, Family of God of gods, the Qualifier of the unqualified, hallelujah! Esther, an orphan from the tribe of Benjamin, had no father and no mother, but her destiny was intact.

Have you ever thought that you don't have anyone to speak for you in high places? Have you wondered how you will get to that place you have desired to be? Have you said like the man at the pool of Bethesda, 'I have no man' **(John 5:7)**; like Mary said, 'I know no man' **(Luke 1:34)**; like Saul said, 'I am the smallest of the least family in Israel' **(1 Samuel 9:21)**; like Gideon said, 'my family is poor in Manasseh' **(Judges 6:15)**? I have good news for you today: you have all it takes to get there. Your Heavenly Father is with you! He is all you need. Esther asked for nothing except that which was necessary; she carried the oil of favor and approached the king. She became queen all by the favor of God.

Saul became King Saul, Mary became the mother of Jesus, Gideon got the victory, the impotent man was healed... all by unmerited favor. Your name is next on this list. You are loved and favored by the King of kings, Lord of lords, Boss of bosses, Governor of all the nations. Get up and go up; you have the Qualifier, your Father with you. You need no man's leg; His leg is the longest (sitting on His throne in heaven, and the earth is His footstool). Luke 1:35 says, 'the Holy Ghost shall come upon you, and the power of the Highest shall overshadow you'. Congratulations, child of God! See you at the top.

PRAYER: *I pray this morning that He will make our feet like the hind's feet and make us walk upon our high places, that we will not lose touch with the presence of God with us today, in the name of Jesus.*

Day 41

Know Your Purpose in Life

Bible Reading: Esther 4:13-17

"For if thou altogether holdest thy peace at this time, then shall there enlargement and deliverance arise to the Jews from another place; but thou and thy father's house shall be destroyed: and who knoweth whether thou art come to the kingdom for such a time as this?" (Esther 4:14).

Good morning, Family of the God who knows the end from the beginning. He is ever faithful, hallelujah! Esther became the queen by the hand of God because He knows the end from the beginning. He saw ahead of her life. He had predestined her before she was born to be the deliverer of the Jews in Shushan.

Brethren, you were not a mistake upon the earth. You did not come into the world by chance, but you were created and sent to the world for a purpose **(Jeremiah 1:5, Luke 1:32-33)**. Your state of origin, residence, job, ministry, position, date of birth, were all planned by our FATHER to fit into the happenings of the time.

There is a purpose that you have been created for, why you are doing what you are doing now, why you are in that position that you are now, why you are where you live now, why you are in that office now, why you are going through what you are going through now. Have you been distracted by so much care that you have forgotten your mission? Have you discovered what your mission is upon the earth, so you can run with it? Esther never knew her mission in the PALACE, but it took Mordecai to show it to her.

What did she do thereafter? She ran with that vision. We sometimes need a "Mordecai" in our journey in life. If you have not discovered the purpose in your life, you need your "Mordecai". The Word of God sent through any vessel can be your "Mordecai". Ask, and it shall be given you; seek, and you shall find; knock, and it shall be opened unto you **(Matthew 7:7)**. Jesus discovered His, and He fulfilled it in style **(Luke 4:18)**. The discovery of your purpose keeps struggles out of your life. You have been ordained for a purpose. Are you complaining about a situation? Is there a battle you are to fight in this hour, and you are nonchalant about it? Is there an unpleasant situation in your environment, and you are not bothered about the deliverance of the people?

Could it be that you are the deliverer sent to deliver your people? Could it be you have been sent as the savior in that family? Could it be you are the intercessor for the moment? Could it be that you are the answer to that family problem? However, I have this truth for you today, "If you refuse to rise up this hour, help will come from another source, but there is a price you will have to pay for neglecting your assignment. God can raise stones to do His bidding, but what God has planned to do, nothing can stop it.

So, brethren, let's rise up and go on that mission, let's rise up and stop the plague, and deliver the oppressed, be the eyes to the blind, hope for the poor, father/mother to the orphans, husband to the widow. What has God called you to do? Stop the complaint, stop the excuses like Esther did. Rise up and fulfill destiny.

PRAYER: *I pray this morning that God will send a "Mordecai" to those who need direction, activate the faith of those who gave up or are giving up on their mission, and send help to us at all levels of our mission in life. We will not fail Him, in the mighty name of Jesus.*

Day 42

Prayer: The Captivity-Turning Key

Bible Reading: Psalm 80:1-14

"Give ear, O Shepherd of Israel, thou that leadest Joseph like a flock; thou that dwellest between the cherubims, shine forth" **(Psalm 80:1).**

Good morning, family of the Shepherd of Israel. He is good, and His mercies endure forever, hallelujah! David turned to God for help. He acknowledged Him as the Shepherd of Israel; he addressed Him with that name.

Brethren, our Lord is our Shepherd, our Father, our Healer, our Provider, the I am that I am. Who do you see Him as? How do you see or rate Him in your heart? Have you seen your life turning the wrong direction, your spiritual life going down, the fire quenching, marriage nose-diving, flourishing business going downward, relationships going sour, health dwindling, ministry in chaos, members going down…? Just name it. What are you doing about it?

Are you saying, "It is well," and doing nothing about it? Are you blaming it on someone or circumstances, or the economy, or the president? Child of God, David in this Psalm knew what to do; He knew there was a Shepherd leading Israel, and he turned to Him. Who do you turn to first when you are challenged? Who do you remember first when you need help? Another sheep like you, another sheep in another sheepfold? A Goat without which is not of the sheepfold? Have we been neglecting our Shepherd to seek help from elsewhere?

This morning, God wants you to know that He is your Shepherd; seek Him first, call upon Him, and He will answer and show you great things which you do not know **(Jeremiah 33:3)**. Ask, and it shall be given **(Matthew 7:7)**. Up till now you have not received because you have not asked; Yes, He knows you are in need of these things, but He will never force Himself on you. He asked blind Bartimaeus what will you have me do for you? **(Mark 10:47-49)**. He responded to the cry of the Israelites in Egypt **(Exodus 3:7)**. Hannah cried, and He answered **(1 Samuel 1:27)**; David cried, and God answered **(Psalm 120:1)**. Cry to our Shepherd, and He will show you the answer, He will show you the man to go to, the way to go, the decision to make to turn your captivity around. Quit looking for help elsewhere; turn to the Shepherd only; He is able and willing and will turn it around for you.

PRAYER: *Father, I pray that we will acknowledge Jesus as our Good Shepherd and learn to put Him first in everything. I pray that as we call today, you will answer and show us the way out of that situation, in Jesus' name.*

Day 43

The Effect of Prayer

Bible Reading: 1 Chronicles 4:1-10

"And Jabez called on the God of Israel, saying, Oh that thou wouldest bless me indeed, and enlarge my coast, and that thine hand might be with me, and that thou wouldest keep me from evil, that it may not grieve me! And God granted him that which he requested" **(1 Chronicles 4:10).**

Good morning, Family of the Unchangeable Changer. He makes all things beautiful in His time, hallelujah!

Jabez was more honorable than his brethren. His mother had given him a name that had shaped his destiny due to the circumstances surrounding his birth. However, Jabez got vexed concerning this and sought the Lord, and He answered him. Prayer changes things.

Have you been called names or a name that has shaped your life? Has the devil tagged you poor, sorrowful, pained, grief, beggar, debtor, sick, troubled, rejected, barren, never-do-well, heartbroken, failure, unsatisfied, unmarried, unhappy...? Whatever name he has tagged you is not permanent. You can change it.

What did Jabez do to be more honorable? He called on the Lord. Have you been called derogatory names? You can say "No, not so," like Elizabeth did **(Luke 1:60)**, like Jacob did with his son Benjamin **(Genesis 35:18)**. Don't sit down and gripe over evil names; don't sit down and accept what God has not spoken concerning you. All Jabez's brothers were mentioned in passing, but He was honored above all of them **(1 Chronicles 4:9-10)**. Arise and change that name; arise and reject that name. Pray like Jacob did, 'I will not Let you go until you bless me **(Genesis 32:26)**. God is waiting to hear you. Pray the prayer of Jabez; "Oh that thou wouldest bless me indeed..."

PRAYER: *Father, we join our faith together to say, No, to evil names. I decree and declare that we are blessed indeed, honorable, lifted, fruitful, glorious, wonderful, accepted, sought out not forsaken, married, lenders, successful, joyous... nothing can change this, for whatever the Lord doeth shall be forever, in the name of Jesus.*

Day 44

It's Not Yet Over

Bible Reading: Jeremiah 20:7-13

> *"But the LORD is with me as a mighty terrible one: therefore my persecutors shall stumble, and they shall not prevail: they shall be greatly ashamed; for they shall not prosper: their everlasting confusion shall never be forgotten"* **(Jeremiah 20:11).**

Good morning, Family of the Covenant-Keeping God. Faithful is He in all the earth, hallelujah! Jeremiah was shut up, but that which God has spoken was not shut up. God's promise upon your life cannot be shut up.

Brethren today, God has sent His word to us saying, "Is anything too hard for the Lord?" Why are you downcast? Why do you think of how God will do it? Quit your calculations; quit pondering on how you will fix it. Mary asked, "How shall this thing be, seeing I know not a man?" **(Luke 1:34).** The king's lord on whose hand the king leaned said, "Even if the Lord will make windows in heaven, might this thing be?" **(2 Kings 7:2).** It shall not be by power nor by might but by His Spirit. You shall not see the rain or the flood, but the valley shall be filled with water.

God did it in the time of Elisha; the famine stopped overnight. Jesus multiplied the 2 fish and 5 loaves in a moment **(Mark 6:41)**. God lifted Joseph from prison to the palace overnight **(Genesis 41:14)**. How did these happen? God sent His word and lifted them and turned their captivity around. Today, you will see your "Hanameel." That which rightfully belongs to you will be handed over to you with evidence. What you never knew was yours will be brought to you. Forget what 'prison' you have been put in. It is your time. Hallelujah!

God cannot lie; Has He said it, He will do it. You shall rise again, you shall stand on your feet again, dust those files again, dust those documents again, pick up those plans again, that ministry plan again, that prayer point again. IT'S TIME.

PRAYER: *Father, in the Name of Jesus, I pray that our Hanameel will bring that which rightfully belongs to us, our lost hope will revive again, our axe head will be found again, our lost glory will be found again. Lord send your captivity-turning word to us as individuals and turn again our captivity in Jesus name.*

Day 45

Acceptable Fast

Bible Reading: Isaiah 58:1-8

***"Withhold not good from them to whom it is due when it is in the power of thine hand to do it"* (Proverbs 3:27).**

Good morning, Family of the Lover of our soul. He wakens us morning by morning; His love is new every morning, and His mercy endures forever. Hallelujah!

Sometimes it feels like God is silent on us. Sometimes you call, and it seems He is far away. The Bible says, "My people perish for lack of knowledge" **(Hosea 4:6)**. God is a God of principles; He is a God of order. How do we fast for speedy answers? Follow God's guidelines for an effective fast. "Loose the bands of wickedness, undo the heavy burden, release the oppressed, break the yokes, feed the hungry, clothe the naked" **(Isaiah 58:6)**. Have you neglected the poor in your midst? Have you turned your back on the needy among you? Do you remember the orphans, the widows, the homeless, your neighbor that has no job, your brother that has no help?

The Bible says, "He that gives to the poor lends to the Lord" **(Proverbs 19:17)**. This is a captivity-turning key; helping the poor. Maybe the prayer you have prayed has the answer in giving a plate of food to that poor orphan, that widow, or that brother in need. Then thou shall call, and He will answer, and your light shall break forth speedily **(Isaiah 58:8-9)**. Reach out, make for that man, woman, or child first, and your break-through shall come upon you and overtake you. Don't turn your back; don't give reasons why you can't give.

There is something you have that the poor need. You are better than millions of beggars in the world. You have what it takes to put a smile on someone's face today. Give substance, give love, give a hug, give a smile, give your last N100, prove God and see. Cornelius gave alms, fasted, and prayed, and His breakthrough came **(Acts 10:31)**. Hear what God said: "Your prayer is heard, and your alms are had in remembrance in the sight of God." Helping the poor is the salt that gives taste to that meal. Let's help the poor and the needy; let's be selfless, and the Lord will come speedily to our help.

PRAYER: *Father, in the name of Jesus, I pray that our eyes will be open to see the riches that you have in stock for us, that we will be empowered to give even our last to the poor, to activate the release of that much that we have been asking for. I pray for the Cornelius spirit to come upon us this morning. We join our faith together to pray for that long-awaited release to come speedily, in Jesus name.*

Day 46

Try Again

Bible Reading: Luke 5:1-12

"And Simon answering said unto him, Master, we have toiled all the night, and have taken nothing: nevertheless at thy word I will" (Luke 5:5).

Good morning, Family of the God who speaks, and the earth obeys. His voice is full of power. Hallelujah!

Brethren, what is your old belief? What have you seen as a norm in your life? Are you still holding onto that belief that you have done everything over the years and nothing has changed? Have you resorted to washing your "nets" and going along with that tide? Our God is a God of times and seasons. I believe this was the worst day in the history of Peter's profession as a fisherman, where no fish was in the sea all night. But could it be that the Creator of the universe had programmed him for this breakthrough; an encounter with destiny in the morning?

Nothing takes God unawares. Peter's encounter with Jesus was not an accident; it was planned before the foundation of the world. The fishes were held back on purpose by our destiny Changer. Have you noticed some dryness and "unanswered" prayers? A change is about to erupt; Jesus is on His way. He had seen your toil; joy is coming in the morning. One encounter with the King of kings will turn that situation around. But how did Peter encounter this breakthrough?

Firstly, he gave his ship for Jesus to SIT DOWN and teach. Have you given a place for Jesus to relax and bless men and bring men to the kingdom? Jesus needs your voice, your home, your vehicle, your money, your knees, your office, your time. What do you have? Give Him willingly for the furtherance of the kingdom, and it will surprise you what He can do for you **(Matthew 6:33)**.

Secondly, Peter forgot his past experience in the night and tried again. Brethren, let that old wine go, forget the former things, behold the new is here. Your unbelief can cost you your breakthrough. Your "bottle" can burst when you bring the past experience and reason with the new instruction.

Believe the word of God absolutely, and it shall come to pass.

PRAYER: *Father in the name of Jesus, I pray this morning that we will wait on the Lord until He comes to get us, I pray that we will surely be delivered out of the hands of the wicked. We claim all your promises; we shall walk in the reality of these promises this week, in Jesus' mighty name.*

Day 47

Not Abandoned

Bible Reading: Psalms 100:1-5

"Know ye that the LORD he is God: it is he that hath made us, and not we ourselves; we are his people, and the sheep of his pasture" **(Psalms 100:3).**

Good morning, Family of the Prince of peace. His covenant cannot be broken, Hallelujah!

Eyes have not seen nor ears heard, nor has it come to the heart of man what God had prepared for them that love Him **(1 Corinthians 2:9).** Let's be reminded that we are HIS FLOCK, the SHEEP of His pasture; we belong to Him. Have you ever felt that you are not important, that you are neglected, forsaken, and hated, no one cares? Brother/Sister, YOU ARE THE CHILD OF THE MOST-HIGH GOD and cannot be abandoned nor forsaken. HE knows your name, loves and cares for you as a person.

Man may abandon you, but the assurance HE has given to us is that He will never leave you nor forsake you **(Matthew 28:20)**. He has given us His promises today, saying: He will feed you, make you lie down, seek that which was lost, strengthen the weak, bring you back to your place of glory and beauty, give you peace, you shall dwell in safety again, send showers of blessing and make you a blessing, the earth shall yield her increase again, none shall make you afraid anymore.

Do you believe the word of God? Your Shepherd is coming for you, and you shall be saved from every harassment of the devil. Rise and take hold of these promises. But to the shepherds who serve not as shepherds but as wolves, God is also coming and will require the soul of every sheep he has given to you to keep. Increase in the number of the flock is great, but are you ready to pay the price for the flock? Every member given to you increases the number of accounts you will give. Feed the flock: feed the lambs and the sheep. His Grace is sufficient; we shall not fail, in Jesus' name.

PRAYER: *Father in the name of Jesus, I pray this morning that we will wait on the Lord until He comes to get us, I pray that we will surely be delivered out of the hands of the wicked. We claim all your promises; we shall walk in the reality of these promises this week, in Jesus' mighty name.*

Day 48

Looking Unto Jesus

Bible Reading: Leviticus 26:1-123

"Ye shall make you no idols nor graven image, neither rear you up a standing image, neither shall ye set up any image of stone in your land, to bow down unto it: for I am the LORD your God" **(Leviticus 26:1).**

Good morning, family of the Lord of lords, the Great I am that I am. He is our God, Hallelujah! It's a great day ahead.

What is God telling us today? "Ye shall make no idols or heaven image or standing image nor set up any image of stone and bow down to it" **(Leviticus 26:1)**. Yes, this is the word of the Lord! You might say, this word is not for me, I am not an idol worshipper and never can be, I am born again and will worship no other god but Jehovah the Almighty. However, severally, we have put our trust, our hope, our confidence in men; father, mother, brother, sister, God-father, mentor, best friend, employer, Mama, Daddy, and things; job, business,.... Who do you first run to, bow to, depend on, believe in, hope on, in the face of challenges? (Even in your mind).

121

Have you idolized any man or thing or job above the Lord our God? Have you been tempted to believe that without someone or a job, you won't make it in life or you can't survive, and you are bowing down to him/her/it? God is telling us today that He is your God. The blessing that accrues to those who trust only in God and put their trust in Him is innumerable. Why don't we repent and trust God to meet all our needs?

He is able. The Bible says "Cursed is anyone that puts his trust in man and maketh flesh his arm, whose heart departeth from the Lord" **(Jeremiah 17:5)**. The reason for that closed heaven may be that you are not truly looking up to the Lord but unto that man, woman, job, business, husband, wife, daughter, son, etc.

Let's repent of our idolatry this morning. On the other hand, if you are in a place of authority, do not make yourself a demi-god. Give all the glory to Him. It's a privilege, render help when necessary, freely you had received from the Lord, freely give **(Matthew 10:8)**.

PRAYER: *I pray that our sins of idolatry be forgiven by the blood of Jesus. I pray that our rain of blessings will begin to fall, our trees shall yield their fruits, we shall eat our bread to the full, we shall chase our enemies that chased us, like Abraham, the Lord shall multiply us beyond our imaginations in all things (Genesis 24:1). Grace to obey his word this morning for these blessings to overtake us is released, in Jesus' name.*

Day 49

Who Is with You?

Bible Reading: Genesis 13:8-15

"And the LORD said unto Abram, after that Lot was separated from him, Lift up now thine eyes, and look from the place where thou art northward, and southward, and eastward, and westward: For all the land which thou seest, to thee will I give it, and to thy seed for ever" **(Genesis 13:14-15).**

Good morning, Family of Wonder-Working God. He is marvelous, Hallelujah!

And the Lord called Abraham alone and blessed him **(Isaiah. 51:2).** God said to Abraham, get thee out of the country and from your father's house to a land which I will show you **(Genesis 12:1).** Lot was not part of the call, why did Abram take Lot?

Brethren, have we taken what God does not include in your journey to destiny? Are there friends, relations, partners, or behaviors, habits that have hindered us from 'seeing' the land that God promised to show to us?

Are we still wandering, searching for that 'land of promise' because there is someone or something that sentiment has brought on our journey of life. It's time to separate from Lot! Search out for the Lot in your life (Please, note that Lot was not evil but was not a part of God's agenda for Abram's life).

There are places we will never reach, positions we will never get to, blessings we will never see, glory we will never experience, success we will never attain if Lot is still in our life. The Word of God tells us in Genesis 13:14 "And the Lord said to Abram, AFTER THAT LOT WAS SEPARATE FROM HIM, lift up NOW your eye and see..." (Emphasis mine). God was silent until Lot was separated from Abraham. Brethren, could it be that the silence you have experienced is the presence of "Lot" in your house, business, life, ministry.

Could it be that God has organized that turbulence for your separation from Lot so He can give you the direction into your glorious destiny? Come out from among them and be ye separate, do away with habits, friends, things that will rob you of your glorious destiny and eternal life. Get rid of that Lot. God is waiting for you, He is waiting with that answer.

PRAYER: *I pray for our eyes to be open to discern who and what Lot is in our lives. I pray that we will locate our promised land, that our blessing will not elude us, our glory will not turn to shame, our beauty will not turn to ashes. We will reach our God-ordained destiny in Jesus' name.*

Day 50

Make Use of the Word

Bible Reading: Joshua 1:3-9

"This book of the law shall not depart out of thy mouth; but thou shalt meditate therein day and night, that thou mayest observe to do according to all that is written therein: for then thou shalt make thy way prosperous, and then thou shalt have good success" **(Joshua 1:8).**

Good morning, Family of God. He wakens us morning by morning to give us the tongue of the learned, hallelujah!

The Word of God today is putting us in remembrance of His word. All things that pertain to life and godliness have been given us. It is our responsibility to discover and take hold of them. How do we do this? Through the knowledge of Christ. Paul says, "that I may know him and the power of his resurrection" **(Philippians 3:10).**

Knowledge comes by hearing and hearing the word of God. Are we neglecting the fellowship of the brethren? Are we neglecting the study of the word of God? We cannot take hold of our inheritance without the knowledge of Him who called us.

Go for the word, reach out and discover what your heritage is in the Book. Your discovery of your heritage leads to the recovery of all that belongs to you. Adding to this faith, virtue, knowledge, temperance, patience, godliness, brotherly kindness, charity (love).

PRAYER: *I pray this morning that we will discover our heritage and recover them, we shall be fruitful and multiply. He will reveal himself to us more than ever before. He will hold us by our hands and lead us into his secret place. Our glory will not turn to shame, our beauty will not fade. For our shame, we shall have double, in mighty Jesus' name.*

Day 51

Avenge Me of My Adversary

Bible Reading: Matthew 18:1-8

"And there was a widow in that city; and she came unto him, saying, Avenge me of mine adversary" **(Luke 18:3).**

Good morning, Family of the God of Vengeance. He has arisen as on Mt. Perazim. Hallelujah!

It's time for war, it's time to rise up and fight for your right. It's time to take your inheritance and stop the wickedness of the wicked. David, in the time of the war of kings, stayed back at home, and he brought pain to the innocent and sinned against God.

This week has been declared our week of divine vengeance, but someone needs to get tired of the oppression, someone needs to call on the Lord. Someone needs to take it by force. The wicked king killed James and stretched forth his hands to take Peter, but the church rose up and said enough is enough, it's not going to be business as usual.

Don't fold your hands and see the hawk pick your chicks one by one and say the Lord knows. You have the power to stop the devil. Gird up yourself, and fight, keep not silence. It is the violent that takes back his stolen goods. The devil does not hear or understand dialogue; He only understands force. God said, if you call, He will answer.

PRAYER: *I join my faith with yours to cry out to the God of vengeance. Every power militating against your growth, success, peace, glory, beauty, increase, your marriage, promotion, job, business, family, meets with the God of Vengeance today. He shall consume them by fire. The Lord thunderbolts into their camp and sets you free in the mighty name of Jesus.*

Day 52

The Lord, My Defence

Bible Reading: Psalma 7:1-15

"If he turn not, he will whet his sword; he hath bent his bow, and made it ready" **(Psalms 7:12).**

Good morning, Family of the Lord our Defender. He has whet His sword; He has bent His bow and made it ready, Hallelujah!

Why do the heathens rage and the people imagine a vain thing, the kings of the earth set themselves together against the Lord and against His Anointed saying let us break their bands asunder and cut his cord from us but He that seated in the heavens shall laugh **(Psalm 2)**. Anything that has a beginning has an end.

The end of wickedness in your life has come. They have fought, they have pulled you down, they have caused you to shed tears, they have said "where is your God?" You have been mocked at, looked down upon, despised. They have planned to take you away, push you aside, mar your destiny. They covered your star and turned your glory to shame. They have ridden on your horse while you are walking on foot, they have sat on your throne while you have been made a servant, a beggar wallowing in poverty, lack, and want. Enough is enough!! Their cup is full, their end has come.

The Judge of the Earth has risen with the instrument of death in his hands to defend and deliver His children. He has appointed over them these four; sword to slay, dogs to rend, fowls of the heaven, and beasts of the earth to devour and destroy **(Jeremiah 15:3)**. Arise and Shout! God goes up with a shout **(Psalms 47:5)**. Arise and praise the Lord! It is an instrument of vengeance **(Psalms 149)**. This is no time to cry and doubt; Get up, your salvation cometh. If God has spoken this morning, He will do it. Swing to action for the bow is made ready to destroy.

PRAYER: *Father in the Name of Jesus, I join my faith with yours this morning and decree an end to every wickedness, to every slavery, every mediocrity. I take back our throne, I take back our horses, I take back our destiny. I decree that in this month God will prove Himself, our captivity will turn as the streams in the South, in the Mighty name of Jesus.*

Day 53

Faith Is the Key

Bible Reading: Hebrews 11:1-6

"Now faith is the substance of things hoped for, the evidence of things not seen" **(Hebrews 11:1).**

Good morning, Family of the Faithful God! He is the God of all possibilities, Hallelujah!

Faith is the substance of things hoped for, the evidence of things not seen **(Hebrews 11:1)**. Bishop David Oyedepo defines faith as "the living force, drawn from the living word, for a living proof." Also defined it as "the currency used to purchase anything from heaven." How long will you cry, how long will you be faithless? How long will you blame God for not delivering you out of your predicament? The day you truly believe is the day of your deliverance. God can and is willing to deliver you, and is coming your way, but when HE cometh shall he find faith? **(Hebrews 18:8).**

We need faith to receive the sent word, to triumph, to be delivered from our enemies, for our healing, and to overcome the wiles of the enemy **(Ephesians 6: 16)**. Without faith, it is impossible to please God, for he that cometh to him MUST believe that He is and is a rewarder of them that diligently seek him **(Hebrews 11:6)**. Is your word of deliverance spoken waiting at your doorstep, have you received the sent word as a child will do, or are you logical about it? Are you weighing the Word in a scale and weighing the vessel used to deliver the Word to you? It is not by might, nor by power but the deliverance is coming by the Spirit.

The Holy Spirit may decide to use a child, your helper, a man of God, a brother... Whoever HE decides to use is not important but have faith in the sent word. That word will not return void but will accomplish that which it has been sent. But when will you believe? Even now. The blind man with his faith handy received his sight IMMEDIATELY **(Luke 18:43)**. The disciples could not calm the storm because of their "LITTLE faith" **(Matthew 8:26)**. The Syrophoenician woman received her request because of her GREAT faith **(Mark 7:24-30)**. Abraham received Isaac because of his STRONG faith **(Romans 4:20)**.

What is your level of faith? It is not God that is holding unto your deliverance. It is your faith that is not on the line. Do you lack faith to receive your request? Go for the word of God concerning the issue and go ask again, for faith comes by hearing and hearing by the word of God **(Romans 10:17)**. The Word of God is the faith booster. God is not unjust to forget your labour. Arise and take responsibility. That answer must come, that vengeance must be repaid, that light must shine forth in your darkness, that destiny must be turned, that breakthrough must come, that turn around must come, that healing must come now.

PRAYER: *Father, in the name of Jesus, I pray that our faith will be built up, that the Author and Finisher of our faith will send help to us. We will not give up until we get to the top, we will not give* *up until the testimony is accomplished, our faith will not fail us. Today, we will believe absolutely, today is the day of our deliverance in the name of Jesus.*

Day 54

Engage Praise

Bible Reading: Psalms 149:1-9

"To execute upon them the judgment written: this honour have all his saints. Praise ye the LORD" **(Psalms 149:9).**

Good morning, Family of the Wonder-Working God who inhabits the praises of His people. May His name alone be praised, Hallelujah!

Have you been saved, given the power to become the son of God, adopted into the beloved, and made righteous by our Lord Jesus Christ? Then you are a saint. Jesus has imputed His righteousness upon us through His death upon the cross. He has qualified us as heirs to His kingdom, reigning with Christ.

There is an honour we do not know that had been given to us by our Father, but most of us do not engage it. The Bible says, *"He who is in honour and does not understand it is as a beast that perisheth"* **(Psalms 47:20).** It also says, *"My people are destroyed for lack of knowledge"* **(Hosea 4:6).** God has put a weapon of PRAISE in our hands to execute judgement, take vengeance, dish out punishments, bind the kings with chains and execute any judgement written in the word **(Psalms 149)**.

Do you know how to dance, sing, clap your hands and play an instrument to praise God? Then you can turn any situation around, stop any enemy in your life, bind any devil oppressing you and teach the enemy a lesson in his life. The devil rides on our ignorance **(Hosea 4:6)**. You have all it takes to defeat him. This honour is given to ALL the saints, including you, yes you! You that had been beaten and battered oppressed. Yes, you who had gone through pain and heartbreak, you whose life's circumstances have conquered.

Break forth into singing **(Isaiah 54:1)**. Pick up your two-edged sword; that is the weapon; it is in your mouth, activate that weapon and begin to use it against your enemy. Don't let him take away your joy anymore and keep you in bondage. Activate your mouth, and let's execute vengeance upon our enemy this morning.

PRAYER: *Father, in the name of Jesus, open our eyes to see this honour. I pray that we will use this sword to destroy the works of darkness and stop the devil's activities in our lives. As Jehoshaphat conquered the people of Moab, Ammon and Mount Seir (2 Chronicle 20:18-25), we will conquer all that comes against us. Let them begin to fight themselves and help destroy one another. Let their "dead bodies" fall to the earth. Help us gather the spoil, both riches and honour. Help us return rejoicing, bringing our sheaves with us, singing songs of victory this month, in Jesus' name.*

Day 55

You Are in Charge

Bible Reading: Genesis 1:27-31

"And God blessed them, and God said unto them, Be fruitful, and multiply, and replenish the earth, and subdue it: and have dominion over the fish of the sea, and over the fowl of the air, and over every living thing that moveth upon the earth" (Genesis 1:28).

Good morning, Family of our Excellent God. He is worthy of praise in all the earth. Hallelujah! God of wonders is yet to do marvellous things again. He has given us a name above all names, that at the mention of the name of Jesus, every knee bows. He has put everything under our feet.

Knowing who you are will put you in control of all the affairs in life. It will keep you far from fear and insecurity and dissolve every impossibility around you. The Bible says you are made a little lower than the angels, and everything is under your feet. Whatever thing changes itself to any form of animal around you has no power over you.

Have you seen yourself being afraid of cats, bats, rats, owls, cockroaches, spiders and the web or whatever animals? Fear not! All the beasts of the earth, fowls of the air, and fish of the sea are under your feet. Take dominion over them by invoking the name of Jesus without fear. We have dominion; it's time to activate this dominion to destroy the works of the enemy. Fear not, give God praise, exalt His holy name. He is a wonder-working God; call him by His name.

Have a superior mentality, be transformed, and renew your mind. Know who you are in Christ, and all impossibility will become possible. All fear will melt away. All difficulties will become nothing before you. All mountains will be levelled. All valleys will be raised. All crooked paths will be made straight a highway to your prepared future will be set for you.

FEAR NOT. You are bigger than that problem, wiser than all your problems.

PRAYER: *I pray that you make us believers of the word of God concerning us, believe in ourselves and receive the word of God to us in faith daily. I delete every wrong picture painted in our minds by the devil. I wipe by the blood of Jesus the handwriting of the devil in our minds. I write upon it the word of God concerning us and implant in our hearts pictures painted from the scriptures by the Holy Ghost, in the name of Jesus.*

Day 56

The Believer's Authority

Bible Reading: Colossians 2:1-12

"We were buried with Him and we have risen with Christ to sit at the right hand of the Father" (Colossians 2:12).

Good morning, Family of the risen King. He is risen, Hallelujah! Have you pondered this word in Colossians 2:12, *"we were buried with Him and we have risen with Christ to sit at the right hand of the Father"*? He raised us from the dead with Christ. Now, we sit with Him at the right hand of the Father. That is the place of authority.

We have the power and authority in Christ to live a supernatural life, live above sin, sickness, poverty, lack and want. Having this authority is one thing and exercising it is another. We have the authority to tread upon serpents, cast out demons, raise the dead, and heal the sick, but our unbelief has robbed us of this power.

Dare to believe, and begin to be on the go for Christ. You have all the power at your disposal as a redemptive right. Arise and begin to exercise it.

What you are looking for is within you, embedded in you, and resides within you. Activate this power, and you will begin to live a triumphant life.

The tomb of Jesus is empty. You were there with Him. The stone of limitation rolled away. Why are you still searching for who will roll the stone away? Look again; that stone before you is a mirage.

The Lord has sent His word to you, saying, "Get up, go back there. That stone's rolled away, you will need no one to help you, but your help has already been sent ahead of you. The stone has been rolled away. That situation has been settled. You will be amazed at what the Lord has done".

PRAYER: *I pray that we will not see those limitations anymore, that suddenly our fears shall be dissolved, and that what we thought we had lost forever will return to us in a more glorious form in Jesus' name.*

Day 57

Know Your Calling

Bible Reading: 1 Peter 1:10

"Wherefore the rather, brethren, give diligence to make your calling and election sure: for ye do these things, ye shall never fall" **(2 Peter 1:10).**

Good morning family of God, He is faithful. To everything, there is a season, and there is time for everything under the earth **(Ecclesiastes 3:1).** Our God is a God of purpose. Nothing takes him by surprise. He saved you so you could be a saviour and taught you so you could be a teacher. He gave you talents to use for the benefit of another. Freely have you received freely give. Selfishness is not a virtue in the kingdom.

Andrew met Christ and returned to bring his brother Simon **(John 1:40-41).** The woman of Samaria met Jesus, and she went and got the whole city (John 4:27-30). Paul taught Priscilla and Aquilla, and they took Apollos and expounded the word to him, resulting in the salvation of more souls **(Acts 18:26).** What have you done with the salvation you received? Are you using it for selfish reasons or getting other souls into the kingdom and strengthening the brethren? A soul you speak to today may be the one that will bring millions into the kingdom. This kingdom has no competition; we are all working towards one goal.

Discover your calling, where it is and who He has sent you to. He sent Paul to the Gentiles and had the backing of Jesus **(Acts 18:6, 9-10)**. Are you sent to the rich, the poor, the downcast, the prostitutes, the widows, children, boys, women, and men? Are you an encourager of the brethren? What message has He given to you? Locate your placement in the kingdom and go for it. Lack of knowledge of where He sent us, when we are to go, our mission and our audience bring competition, envy and disharmony among churches.

Everyone is called for a particular assignment and sent to specific people (over seven billion humans are on the earth). Stars in the sky don't struggle to shine and do not struggle for space. Get rid of competition, get rid of envy, get rid of talking down on your brethren, and encourage the brethren that are coming up strong. There is a blessing waiting for you.

Souls out there are waiting for you. Millions are waiting in the valley for a decision. Can you rescue them from hell and bring them to Jesus? Not for self-aggrandizement or selfish interest but for love for Jesus and the kingdom. The struggle will cease when you locate where you are and who He sent you to.

PRAYER: *I pray we will locate our calling and pursue it with all our hearts. I come against every spirit of competition, envy and comparison. I pray for the Lord to send help our way today. I pray that we will catch that goldfish today for Jesus, and our reward will come speedily in Jesus' name.*

Day 58

All You Need Is in The Word

Bible Reading: John 1:1-5

"All things were made by him; and without him was not any thing made that was made" **(John 1:3).**

Good morning, Family of Jehovah Jireh. Blessings, honour, and glory be to His forever, hallelujah!!

Who is the man that fears the Lord? It is he that does His commandment. The fear of the Lord is the beginning of wisdom, knowledge, and to depart from evil **(Proverb 1:7)**. What are you chasing after? Riches, honour, children, wealth, blessing...? You can find all of these things in the word of God. The word of God has the principles to allow you to obtain all these things. You have searched for them elsewhere for too long. Look inward.

The Bible says, *"lo, I come in the volume of books that is written of me."* Jesus located the secret and became the most successful **(Luke 4:18)**.

David says in Psalms 1, *"Blessed is the man that walks not in the counsel of the wicked.... but his delight is in the law of the Lord... he shall be like a tree planted by the rivers of water."* That is success!

In Joshua 1:8, the Bible says, *"This book of the law shall not depart out of thy mouth, but thou shall meditate upon it day and night... then thou shall have good success."*

Everything you are looking for is in the Book. You can have them at your disposal, but you must first DELIGHT greatly in His commandment **(Psalms 112:1, Psalms 1:2, Joshua 1:8)**.

Pick up that word daily, study and meditate upon it. And everything that belongs to you will begin to chase after you. Remember, you are what you eat; God's word is Himself. You become God when you eat HIM daily. God is not in need. He cannot be molested. He cannot be pushed aside. He is not poor. He is not sick. Let the word of God be your daily diet, and you will find rest for your soul.

Goodness and mercy, riches and honour will begin to chase after you and overtake you. Before you call, God will answer. While you are yet speaking, he will hear, and your heart's desire will come to pass speedily. I pray that the zeal to study the word will come upon us. As we are not too busy to eat our physical food, surely, we need to eat out spiritual food.

PRAYER: *I pray for the Spirit of God to quicken our mortal bodies and for every weariness and slumber to be destroyed in us. Arise and possess your possession in Jesus' mighty name.*

Day 59

A Heart That Fears God

Bible Reading: Psalms 112:1-5

"Praise ye the LORD. Blessed is the man that feareth the LORD, that delighteth greatly in his commandments" **(Psalms 112:1).**

Good morning, Family of the King of kings and the Lord of lords. His mercy is new every morning, hallelujah! He sent His word and healed and delivered from shame. Who is the man that fears the Lord? It is he that departs from evil and obeys his commandment. The fear of the Lord is to hate evil: arrogance and pride, and the evil way and fraudulent mouth **(Proverbs 8:13)**. Have you gone around in circles for so long? Are we seeking which way to go? The fear of the Lord will lead us on the way to go **(Psalms 25:12)**.

God's promised blessings for us might not be fulfilled if we disregard His commands. The beginning of your blessings is in departing from evil. This week God has kept great blessings ahead of us. However, we must drop that weight, that fraudulent activity, those works of iniquity, that hypocrisy, that secret sin, that envy, that jealousy, that revenge, those filthy thoughts, that anger, that unforgiveness that has lingered for years, that bitterness, that oppression of the poor around you, that gossip, and that evil addiction **(Galatians 5:19)**. Yes, what is yours no one can take but remove that barrier **(Isaiah 59:1)** and all these blessings will begin to drop on you in abundance.

PRAYER: *Father, in the name of Jesus, we pray that you pour the spirit of the fear of the Lord upon us to activate the release of blessings upon our lives: we shall eat the labour of our hands, and it shall be well with us, our children shall be like the olive tree round about us, you shall be blessed out of Zion, and shall see the good of this land. You shall not die but shall live to see your children's children in the name of Jesus.*

Day 60

The Power of Praise

Bible Reading: Psalms 67:5-7

"Then shall the earth yield her increase; and God, even our own God, shall bless us" **(Psalms 67:6).**

Good morning, Family of God, the Maker of the heavens and the earth. Our God reigns forever and ever. Hallelujah!

Life without Christ is full of crises. Life without direction is full of frustration. But we have a Shepherd who guides and shows us where to go. Hallelujah! We owe him praise forever. Our Lord Jesus hands us the keys to stress-free living. The discovery of these keys puts man in control of the affairs of life. Praise is a weapon against the enemy **(Psalms 149)**. Today the same weapon is shown as an instrument of multiplication **(Psalms 67:6-7)**. Praise brings increase, and more praise brings fearful blessings **(Psalms 67:7)**.

Have you seen the hand of God in any area of your life? Have you asked for rain and noticed a little cloud forming? Praise Him. Are you asking for bread to feed 5,000 men, and you only have five loaves and two fish? Praise Him! Are you asking for souls to be saved but instead, you have seen yourself - imprisoned as Paul and Silas **(Acts 16:25)**? Praise Him. Is the situation before you looking impossible, like Lazarus in the tomb **(John 11: 41-43)**? Praise Him. Is that the last meal for you and your children? Praise Him!

Are your creditors coming for you and your properties? Praise Him. Is that mountain before you higher than you to surmount? Praise Him! Is the red sea in front of you, and you can't cross it? Praise Him! Are the enemies joined together, coming after you to destroy you **(2 Chronicles 20:20-22)**? Praise Him!

Praise is a multiplier, a magnifier. Praise activates the hand of God to work on your behalf. God has sent His word to us, PRAISE HIM, AND THE EARTH SHALL YIELD ITS INCREASE. You don't need to beg, worry, shed tears, ask questions, murmur and complain. PRAISE HIM. This commandment is for our glorification **(Leviticus 26:4-12)**.

Your due season has come, your rain of blessing is falling, your land shall yield its increase, your threshing shall reach into vintage, the vintage shall reach sowing time, you shall eat your bread to the full, you shall begin to chase your enemies, the Lord shall have respect unto you and multiply you exceedingly in the mighty name of Jesus. GOD CANNOT LIE.

PRAYER: *I pray that we receive the garment of praise and that your promise to us will come to pass as we praise you in Jesus' name.*

Day 61

It's Your Time

Bible Reading: Isaiah 60:1-22

"Arise, shine; for thy light is come, and the glory of the LORD is risen upon thee" **(Isaiah 60:1).**

Good morning, sons and daughters of the Most-High God. The God that made times and seasons. He is worthy! Hallelujah! It's a new day. It's a day of shining. It's a day of fulfilment of prophecies. It's a day of visitation. It's a day of rejoicing for them that dare to believe. Arise and shine. Your light has come; darkness is over. It's a different day.

Have you been afflicted and hated so that no man went through you? Your season has come. Your due season of visitation has come. The Word of God says, "I will make you an eternal Excellency." Have men despised you? It's not over yet; wait! Their sons are coming to bend down at the sole of your feet. Joseph's word came, and he was loosed from prison chains and made a Prime minister to rule over Potiphar's wife, teach Senators and bind princes at will **(Psalms 105:19-22)**. Ah! God's ways are past finding out!

The darkness may cover the people, but the stage light is upon you now. All eyes are on you. Stand up from the dust, lift your eyes and see. They all gather; they come to you. They shall come from afar in ships, on land, or by air. They are coming! The time of your visitation is here. There is a change of level for you. It's not according to the economy of this world but according to that of heaven.

Are you at the brass level? Gold is coming. Are you at an iron level? Silver is coming. Are you at wood level? Brass is coming. Are you at stones level? Iron is coming. ARISE, lift your eyes and see. God told Abraham as far as your eyes can see, I will give to you. *Jeremiah 1:10-12, He says, "You have well seen, I will hasten my word to perform it".* Verse 10 says, *"SEE. I have this day set you over the nations."* You must first SEE, behold, lift your eyes. See your expectations to actualize it.

PRAYER: *I pray this morning that God will give us the eyes to see and receive His sent word. I come against the thief that stands in our way to steal and confiscate our blessings. I cover our parcels with the blood of Jesus. I wrap it up with fire. It shall reach us swiftly. In the twinkling of an eye, our change will come in the name of Jesus.*

Day 62

Rejoice

Bible Reading: Isaiah 40:1-6

"Comfort ye, comfort ye, my people, says the Lord. Speak ye comfortably to Jerusalem and cry, that her warfare is accomplished, that her iniquity is pardoned, for she shall receive of the Lord's hands double for all her sins" **(Isaiah 40:1-2).**

Good morning, Children of the merciful God. His mercy endures forever, Hallelujah!

Have you been afflicted? Have you been in "pain' for years and months? have you had an issue of long continuance? Does your wound appear incurable? Have you cried and pleaded, and it seems God is far away? Have your lovers and your praise singers forgotten you? Weep not; the book is opened today. It may be a day of gloominess for others, but God says, He will save you from it.

Men will say there is a casting down, but you will say there is a rising up. The darkness shall cover the earth, but light shall shine upon thee. The plagues shall come upon the earth, but your land shall be as Goshen. Fear not! for out of you shall proceed thanksgiving. The Lord shall restore your health and heal your wounds. Multiplication is your portion this season. He shall turn your captivity like He did Job **(Job 42:10-12)**. Your latter end shall be greater than the former. He is lifting that burden out of your neck. You shall be termed a city sort out, not forsaken. Why do you ask, how this shall be? Nothing is too hard for Him. Nothing is too late for Him, and nothing is incurable with Him. He is the Supreme God.

He called Abraham at 75. He made Sarah a mother at 90. He healed Job and restored his fortune suddenly. He made Mary give birth as a virgin. He brought water out of the rock. He made the walls of Jericho fall with trumpets. He made Joseph a prisoner/ foreigner to become a Prime minister. He divided the Red Sea with a rod. He made Elijah outrun a Chariot and fed him with a raven. He fed 5,000 men with two fish and five loaves of bread. He raised Lazarus from the dead. Are you still doubting what He can do suddenly? He is more than able to do what He says He will do. Be expectant, get the pots for the increase of the oil, expand the place of your tent, and prepare your victuals **(Joshua 1:11)** for you are crossing that river. It is your season. It is your time!!!

Don't listen to the happenings around you. Jesus is undoubtedly coming soon, but where will HE find you? In pain or depression, or with joy serving the Lord. This message spread abroad. The message of health and wealth, and prosperity. Awake, Awake, get ready. It's the time of our crossing over, from sickness to health, from poverty to riches, from mediocrity to celebrity, from smallness to glory, from fewness to multiplication, from little to thousand.

PRAYER: *I pray this morning that we will believe the Lord, be willing and obedient, and eat the good of this land. I pray for the mercy of the Lord to locate us from today and confirm His word in our lives in Jesus' name.*

Day 63

Believe in Yourself: You Can Do It

Bible Reading: Genesis 1:1-31

" ¹ In the beginning, God created the heaven and the earth.

² And the earth was without form, and void; and darkness was upon the face of the deep. And the Spirit of God moved upon the face of the waters" **(Genesis 1:1-2).**

Good morning, Family of Our CREATOR. Great are you, Lord, forever. Hallelujah!

The Spirit of the Lord moved upon the face of the waters **(Genesis 1)**. God created heaven and earth; however, the earth was challenged; void, formless, and darkness were the order of the day. God did not abandon the earth; He did not look hopeless because He had the solution to the challenges of the earth. We are made in the likeness of God. We are the image of our God.

Are you challenged? Is everything you try to do not taking shape (form-less)? Do you feel empty and see your life on a zero level? Are you not seeing headway in your plans because the darkness has covered everywhere? I come with good news this morning; God went through the same situation, and the solution is in His word. He has given us a template in Genesis 1. See how He brought a solution to HIS challenges:

1. His spirit came into play, meditating until the word came.
2. He brought light and separated it from the darkness.
3. He began speaking daily about what he wanted to see. He did this in stages, separating in order the earth, the firmament, and the waters and filling them.
4. He spoke some things to being, and he MADE some.
5. He saw everything that HE spoke. His expectations came to pass, and the challenges of voidness, formlessness and darkness were over.

Do you want instant testimonies? Sometimes you need to take your challenges in stages and deal with them. God has given you the power. Go for knowledge (light), switch on this light and go to work. God restored the dry bones in Ezekiel 37 in stages. Ezekiel prophesied as he commanded, and the army was restored. Jesus, when feeding the 5,000, first told them to sit in groups of 50, and they were fed. God gave you the power and the brain (His mind), so you can work things out. Break down your challenges and begin to prophesy what you want to see. God has released the angels to help, but you must take responsibility as sons, not children. Rise, and deal with that problem. Give God praise for the success of the day. God daily assessed and saw that everything He made was good. The answer to that problem is within you. Get up and get working!!!

PRAYER: *Father, in the name of Jesus, I pray that the Spirit of the Lord will move over our challenges and empower us to overcome them. I pray for the wisdom of God that creates to come upon us as we rise and face our challenges in stages today. We will not fail*

Him. Our CREATOR will be proud of us this season; I pray that our voidness, formlessness and darkness will be over in the mighty name of Jesus.

Day 64

Activate the Spirit of Praise

Bible Reading: Psalms 30:1-12

"Sing unto the LORD, O ye saints of his, and give thanks at the remembrance of his holiness" **(Psalms 30:4).**

Good morning, Family of God. He is good, and His mercy endures forever, Hallelujah!!! *"Weeping may endure for a night, but joy cometh in the morning"* **(Psalm 30:5).** Think about this! Do you believe in your heart that this is true? Are you seeing your mourning turned to dancing? Then it's time to forget old things and make preparations for the new that is coming. *"Remember not the former things behold I do a new thing shall you not see it. I will even make a way in the wilderness and rivers in the desert"* **(Isaiah 43:18-19).** We have not thanked Him enough for what He has done and is doing. We are so behind in our praise to Him. David, a man after God's heart, often returned to sing the praises of God for every victory he won, every answer to prayers, every protection and guidance. He won the heart of God. These acts gave him access to the world of victories **(Psalms 119:164).**

How Do You Activate The Spirit Of Praise Amid Chaos And Trouble?

1. Think back at your past victories, the last answer to prayers, help, favours etc. And begin to praise the Lord **(Exodus 15)**.
2. Think of your glorious future backed by the promises of the Lord to His children. Create your picture of your future from the scripture, and joy and merriment will break forth from your heart. Songs of praise will cast all depression and hurt away **(Luke 1: 46-49)**.

PRAYER: *Father, in the name of Jesus, I pray that we will see the reasons to praise you, O Lord. Every reason for depression is destroyed today. Our comfort season has arrived, and the dawning of a new day is here, in Jesus' name.*

Day 65

Wait, Change Is Coming

Bible Reading: Genesis 26:1-5

"And the LORD appeared unto him, and said, Go not down into Egypt; dwell in the land which I shall tell thee of" **(Genesis 26:2).**

Good morning, Family of the ever-present God, He never sleeps. He never slumbers. Hallelujah! *"And thine ear shall hear a word behind you saying, this is the way walk ye in it..."* **(Isaiah 30:21).**

Brethren, God speaks all the time but are you listening to Him or the voice of your body? The Bible says, *"trust in the Lord with all your heart and lean not unto your own understanding..."* But we sometimes take counsel from our expertise and trust in the arm of flesh. That plan to go down to "Egypt" for help, did the Lord direct you there? Have you asked His counsel concerning that issue at hand? Are you seeking help from them that are ashamed of you as a child of God? **(Isaiah 30:5).** The Lord is saying to you, "Go not down to Egypt for help, wait". Seek help from the Lord:

1. Return to Him and be at rest.
2. Be quiet and confident to hear Him speak to you.
3. Exalt the name of the Lord as the Shepherd of your soul.
4. Wait for Him!! **(Isa. 30:15-18)**.

A change can only come to them that wait upon the Lord. Isaac waited, obeyed, and became an envy of the Philistine **(Genesis 26:12-14)**. Abraham waited and became a father of many nations **(Romans 4:20)**. David waited and recovered all he lost **(1 Samuel 30:7-9, 18)**. Wait! Be quiet, return to the Lord, and you shall hear a voice behind you saying, "this is the way; walk ye in it". They that wait upon the Lord shall renew their strength. Though He tarries, wait for Him. He will go with you if He sends you. God's presence is all you need to succeed.

PRAYER: *I pray that the grace to wait to hear Him be granted to us. We will not be like Saul, who lost his throne to impatience. We come against every spirit that wants to push us to destruction; we shut our ears to the voice of the enemy. We pray for our ears to hear only HIM as we wait upon Him in the mighty name of Jesus.*

Day 66

Enter into Your Rest

Bible Reading: Hebrews 4:1-3

"For unto us was the gospel preached as well as into them but the word preached did not profit them not being mixed with to them that heard it. For we which have BELIEVED do enter into rest ..." **(Hebrews 4:2-3).**

Good morning, Chosen Children of God. His love is new every morning. Hallelujah!!!

Brethren, there is a place of rest where access is granted only by faith. But how many have entered therein? A place of peace, of no struggle, a place of abundance, a place where all things are possible. The realm where God dwells. Solomon entered there **(1 Kings 5:4)**, and Abraham entered there **(Genesis 24:1)**.

We have struggled all our lives because of ignorance of who we are and God's will for our lives, because of fear, unbelief and logical (carnal) thinking which is predominant in the system of this world. Happenings around us have corrupted our minds: fear, logic, what we hear, and limitations of the design of this world. These things control our five senses. We need a system reset. A little child does not know fear or impossibilities. He believes all things are possible if he asks. He enters anywhere he wishes. But as he grows up, the world system puts limitations, boundaries, and nos and don'ts, and he loses that mind.

Jesus says if we do not receive the kingdom as a child, we cannot enter it **(Mark 10:15)**. We need a mental transformation. We need to activate the mind of Christ if we want to enter into the rest of God. God created the world in 6 days and rested on the 7th day **(Genesis 2:2)**. Since then, nothing has been added but discovered **(Ecclesiastics 1:9)**. Everything revolves around that God created. He has made all things that pertain to your life and has stored them for you, but you need to discover them to recover them **(2 Peter 1:3)**. But you cannot do this with a carnal mind. How do we enter that rest which remains for the people of God **(Hebrew 4:9)**?

Believe!!! Believe that all things, whatsoever you ask, when you pray, you receive it **(Mark 11:23-24)**. Destroy doubt, fear and impossibility thinking; these will rob you of your inheritance. ALL things are possible to them that believe **(Mark 9:23)**. Arise, enter your rest, speak your desire to being and believe that you have received it, and you shall have it.

PRAYER: *I pray that the Lord will reset our minds. I pray that we will enter that rest that He has kept for us and that He shall recover everything belonging to us that we lost this season and that He shall destroy our doubts and unbelief. Our rest has come, and our struggles have ended in the name of Jesus.*

Day 67

Every Success Experience Has a Story

Bible Reading: 2 Corinthians 6:1-5

"We then, as workers together with Him beseech you also that ye receive not the grace of God in vain" **(2 Corinthians 6:1).**

Good morning, Family of the Good Shepherd, who leads his children into all truth. Praise Jesus!!

Working with the Master was not designed to be smooth at all times. Going on a long journey has its ups and downs, and the work of the ministry is no different. There are mountains to climb, rivers to cross, devils to deal with, men to understand, problems to solve, and sleepless nights of prayer. Paul in 2 Corinthians 6 spells out challenges experienced in ministry: trying your patience, afflictions, distress, stripes, imprisonment, labour, watching, fasting, chastening, poverty, dishonour, calling of names, scourging tongues of men etc. Are you in ministry and expecting to have it smooth?

No matter what level of ministry you are involved in, you need to know that there is a cross to carry. There is a story behind the success, a scar behind the star, and a price behind the prize. Are you willing to be used by God to do many exploits and much more exploits? Get ready to pay the price. Are you prepared to excel in whatever area God has called you? Then, you need to be prepared to pay the price. EVERY SUCCESS EXPERIENCE HAS A STORY.

Don't be afraid of the pain you are going through now. Don't be frightened by the rejections, the separations, the wilderness experience, the basements. Moses, the "Prince of Egypt", went through the wilderness and Jethro's house for 40 years because he had a great ministry ahead **(Exodus 2:15-25)**. David was with the sheep in the wilderness, facing the lion and the bear, running in bushes, learning to dodge the enemy, but he got trained for the great job ahead. Paul went through all his sufferings because he had two-thirds of the New Testament to write. Jesus went through the cross because he had the world to save.

The "suffering" you are facing might not be the devil but a preparation for your throne and great ministry ahead of you. The devil is not stronger than God! God is the Master and Architect of your life. You are peculiar. You are different. Separate yourself from others. Your call is not to the same people. Your call is not to shepherd the same flock. You are not sent to the same people. Know who you are and who has sent you. You have a great destiny! Hold His hand and let him lead you.

PRAYER: *Father, in the name of Jesus, I pray this morning that we will never accuse God of our challenges. We pray for the eyes to see ahead to judge him faithful who has called us. Let the enabling power of God engrace us afresh, never to give up at the brink of our turn around, in Jesus' name.*

Day 68

Refuse to Give Up

Bible Reading: 2 Kings 2:1-14

"And Elijah said unto Elisha, Tarry here, I pray thee; for the LORD hath sent me to Bethel. And Elisha said unto him, As the LORD liveth, and as thy soul liveth, I will not leave thee. So they went down to Bethel" (2 Kings 2:2).

Good morning, Children of the rewarder God. He rewards those who diligently seek Him. Hallelujah!

Sometimes, the journey to getting our heart's desire seems too long. Some give up on the way, and some turn back, giving reasons. Have you desired anything from God? Have you prayed for years, months or weeks, and it seems the answer is far-fetched? I tell you the truth; God rewards diligence. The prize for a marathon race goes to the one that persists to the end. Elisha desired the double portion of the anointing of his master Elijah, and he got it at the end **(2 Kings 2:13)**. Jacob desired a blessing and a change of story, and he got it at the end **(Genesis 32:26-29)**. Ruth chose to be with Naomi, and she got rewarded at the end **(Ruth 1:17, 4:13)**. Bartimaeus desired his sight back, but he refused to be discouraged and got it at the end (**Mark 10:47-51**). How did they get their desires met?

1. They refused to be discouraged.

• To Jacob, the Angel said, "Let me go for the day breaketh and he said, *"I will not let you go except you bless me"* (**Genesis 33:26**).

• To Ruth, Naomi said, *"Turn again my daughter and go your way for I am too old to have a husband... behold your sister- In-law is gone back..."* and Ruth said, *"Entreat me not to leave you or to return from following after thee..."* (**Ruth 1:16**).

• To blind Bartimaeus, many charged him that he should hold his peace, but he cried a great deal, *"Thou Son of David have mercy on me"* (**Mark 10:48**).

• To Elisha, Elijah said, *"Tarry here, for the Lord has sent me to Bethel,"* but he said, *"As the Lord liveth and as thy soul liveth, I will not leave thee"* (**2 Kings 2:2**).

What are you saying? Are you still giving up? Are you still washing your net? Are you throwing in the towel? Or are you saying, " I will not leave you except you bless me"?

2. They refused to be distracted; they remained focused on their dream. Elisha said, "Yea, I know, hold your peace" (**2 Kings 2:3**).

3. They persisted to the end. 2 Kings 2:9, *"Ask what I shall do for thee..."* *"What is thy name?"* (**Genesis 32:27**). "What will thou that I should do unto thee?" (**Mark 10:51**). *"Who art thou?"* (**Ruth 3:9**).

Persist until you hear His voice speak to you. DO NOT GIVE UP!!!! Mockers and detractors are part of the success stories of great men. If they do not mock, you cannot be made.

They don't only appear on your way to success to distract you but appear again when you have been changed to bow before you. Don't give up like Orpah. There is a reward waiting for you. Elisha returned a changed man, full of power, became lord over his mockers and detractors, became a solution carrier and a terror to all forms of mockery.

Don't give up, be persistently constant in your search. As the Lord changed Jacob's name, yours also will be changed. As Ruth became the path to bringing the Saviour to the world, God will also open your destiny. As blind Bartimaeus became the centre of attraction that day, you also will be noticed. As Elisha returned with double anointing, yours will not elude you.

Get up! Don't listen to that deceiver, don't listen to that mocker, and don't reason with that devil to give up. Jesus will stand still and grant you your heart's desire.

PRAYER: *Father, in the name of Jesus, I pray this morning that we will not give up at Bethel or Jericho, but we will cross over this Jordan to get what we have desired. Lord! Shut our ears to the voice of our mockers; help us to focus on the prize of our high calling in Christ in Jesus' name.*

Day 69

Synergize to Gain Victory

Bible Reading: 2 Kings 3:1-17

"And he went and sent to Jehoshaphat the king of Judah, saying, the king of Moab hath rebelled against me: wilt thou go with me against Moab to battle? And he said, I will go up: I am as thou art, my people as thy people, and my horses as thy horses" (2 **Kings 3:7).**

Good morning, Family of the Almighty God. His mercy is new every morning, Hallelujah!

Who you follow determines what follows you. Who are your allies? Who are you walking with?

Who do you run to when you need help? Life is a battle, and you must fight every day to make it. Some battles are more than you can fight on your own. The Bible says, "one can chase one thousand, but two will put 10,000 to flight **(Deuteronomy 32:30)**. Jehoram counted Israel and decided to seek help from Jehosaphat, whose presence in the battle brought them victory. Who do you join forces with? Who are your business associates? Who are your partners in Ministry? Are your enemies their enemies? Are your victories their victories; are your success their success? Jehoshaphat said, "I am as thou art and my people as thy people..." **(2 Kings 3:7)**. It could be that your progress is affected by your associates. How did Jehoram win the battle?

1. He located his challenge (Moab).
2. Weighed his strength (Counted the Israelites) and discovered that he could not fight the battle alone.
3. He sought help from his brother's nation, stronger than he was.
4. When there was no hope, his ally sought the Lord.
5. God took over the battle, and victory was sure.

You can only win the battles of life if you sit down to strategize. Don't live your life carelessly, don't fight your battles alone, seek help from the Lord, and you will be sure of victory. God says, "You have sought me and will find me." "Ye shall not see wind, neither shall ye see rain, yet the valley shall be filled with water... This is a light thing in the sight of the Lord" **(2 Kings 3:17-18)**. Don't lose hope like Jehoram **(2 Kings 2:10)**. There is victory, glory, honour and abundance ahead. His word will not go forth without accomplishing that which it has been sent.

PRAYER: *Father, in the name of Jesus, I pray that our Jehosaphat will be available for us. I pray that God will direct us to our destiny helpers. We will not be led into the wrong hands, and our battles will be won today, in Jesus' name.*

Day 70

Shut the Door to Receive Your Answers

Bible Reading: 2 Kings 4:1-7

"And when thou art come in, thou shalt shut the door upon thee and upon thy sons, and shalt pour out into all those vessels, and thou shalt set aside that which is full" **(2 Kings 4:1-7).**

Good morning, Family of the Miracle-Working God. He is worthy, Hallelujah!

It will be impossible for man to fathom how great our God is without challenges. Lazarus died so that the Resurrection and the Life would show up, the man was lame to reveal the Healer, and the prophet's wife had to be in want for the Multiplier God to multiply the crus of oil.

Are you going through any challenges? Are you facing a situation that is bigger than you? Then, rejoice for the I AM THAT I AM is about to reveal himself to you. He is the Prince of peace, the Healer, the Resurrection and the Life, the Glory and the Lifter up of your head, the Multiplier, the Debt payer, the Banker, your Advocate, the Restorer of the bridge, the Builder.

You can add your situation there! Are you running from pillar to post, trying to find solutions to your problems? He is near you and with you. In the bid to solve their problems, some have aggravated their problems by exposing themselves to the devil, opening the doors to their homes, businesses, marriage etc. The Shunammite woman "Shut the door" behind her problem and went back to the Source of her blessing, The wife of the prophet "shut the door" and poured out the oil as she was instructed **(2 Kings 4:5)**. Elisha "shut the door" and raised the dead son to life **(2 Kings 4:33)**.

To get your miracles, "shut your door" to distractions, shut the door to panic, shut the door and get the word for the season. The word is nigh unto you, even in your mouth. There is a solution waiting for you. You are too troubled. You are too outward-oriented. Look inward. That solution is in your house. The solution is with you. Only if you can "shut the door". Jesus said, "when ye have shut the door, pray" **(Matthew 6:6)**. Great testimonies are delayed, and some miracles never happen because men have not gotten the keys to having them. Shut the door and hold unto the Source until He answers you. The Shunammite woman said, *"As the Lord liveth and as the soul liveth, I will not leave thee..."* **(2 Kings 4:30)**.

I admonish us today to "shut the door" and get back to the Source. He has the solution to that challenge. As the prophet's wife shut the door and opened it with what she asked in her hand, as the Shunammite woman shut the door behind her and opened it receiving her child back alive, and as Elisha shut the door and opened it with the living child, so shall you open that door coming out with the solution in your hands.

PRAYER: *Father, in the name of Jesus, I pray today that the Grace to "shut the door" and wait on the Lord be given to us. The solu-*

tions to our problems will finally come. We will find Him when we call, and our change of story will be in our hands, in Jesus' mighty name.

Day 71

Your Circumstances Do Not Define Who You Are

Bible Reading: 2 Kings 5:1-18

"Now Naaman, captain of the host of the king of Syria, was a great man with his master, and honourable, because by him the LORD had given deliverance unto Syria: he was also a mighty man in valour, but he was a leper" **(2 Kings 5:1)**.

Good morning, Family of the Omniscient God. He is a great God. Praise Jehovah!

The Lord hath chosen the foolish things of this world to confound the wise; and hath chosen weak things of this world to confound the things that are mighty **(1 Corinthians 1:27)**. Naaman, the captain of the host of the King of Syria, was a great man, honourable, and a mighty man of valour BUT he was a leper **(2 Kings 5:1)**.

Do you have a 'but' in your life though everything around you seem to be doing great? Have you tried every avenue to take that "but" away from your life to no avail? Your answer could be where you least expected. Your answer could be in just one word from God through the mouth of His servant **(2 Kings 5:10)**.

The maid of the Naaman's wife was not among the mighty men of Syria, nor among the officers of the Army nor the princes of the land but she had the answer in her. You may not look like it now, but you are the answer to that 'king's' challenge, that company or that family challenge. God does not look at the outward appearance but looks at the heart **(1 Samuel 16:7)**. Your elevation is in that gift that is embedded in you. The gift of a man maketh room for him **(Proverbs 18:16)**.

Have they looked down on you? Have they thought you are a nobody? Have they counted and called men of renown, and you are pushed aside as a nonentity? Cheer up. You might be the carrier of that answer.

The maid of the Wife of Naaman had the answer to Naaman's leprosy **(2 Kings 5:3)**. The little boy had the bread and the fish needed to feed the 5,000 **(John 6:9)**. David was the answer Israel was looking for to conquer Goliath **(1 Samuel 17: 32)**, Solomon the least esteemed among the princes was the answer to Israel's peace and rest **(1 Kings 1:25-26)**, Jephthah, the son of the prostitute was the answer to the wars in Israel **(Judges 11:1-2)**, Joseph the prisoner was the answer to the famine in Egypt **(Genesis 41:34)**, Jordan not Abana or Pharpar was the answer to Naaman's leprosy **(2 Kings 5:12)**.

Are you still looking down on yourself and feeling down? Are you still looking for a way to gain 'fake' riches and honour like Gehazi **(2 Kings 5:20)** instead of being content and working with all your heart in the place of your assignment?

When your time comes, you will be called forth like David, Joseph, Daniel, Solomon, the little boy with lunch, Mary, and the little maid. Fake riches bring leprosy, don't gain the riches with scheming, and lying, don't go up by yourself, and don't let the devil promote you; he will abandon you when you need him most. The promotions that come from the Lord are enduring and honourable.

Wait in your place of assignment. Your day of visitation is loading and shall surely come. Generations after you shall call you blessed.

PRAYER: *I pray that we will not be led astray. I pray that our time of visitation comes speedily. Father, create that problem in the palace of kings that has the answer in us and help us to fulfil our destiny in the name of Jesus Christ.*

Day 72

Serve the Lord with All of You

Bible Reading: Exodus 23:25-31

"And ye shall serve the LORD your God, and he shall bless thy bread, and thy water; and I will take sickness away from the midst of thee" **(Exodus 23:25).**

Good morning, Family of our Living God. Great grace is multiplied unto us. Hallelujah!

Brethren, many are called, but few are chosen **(Mathew 22:14)**. God by grace elected us to serve Him **(1 Thessalonians 1:4)**. We were not qualified to be elected into the service of the King of kings, the Holy God who cannot behold iniquity.

Let's look back at our lives. What qualified you to be chosen above your peers to serve in the palace of the Almighty God? Nothing! It was an election of grace. For your righteousness is as a filthy rag before God **(Isaiah 64:6)**. The scripture says, "to whom much is given, much is required" **(Luke 12:48)**. How are we serving the Master? Have we forgotten that we were elected by grace to serve? Have you lost your zeal because of the cares of life, your career, money, problems that seem not to be solved, or sickness? What can separate us from the love of Christ? **(Romans 8:35-39)**.

The Thessalonican church was commended for their work of faith, their labour of love, and their patience of hope. They did these IN THE SIGHT OF GOD. Not for man to see and applaud. Let's examine ourselves; are you burning with the fire and zeal to serve the Master, or are you only interested in Him servicing your needs?

Different Categories of Servants that are Present in the Church Today:

1. Those that serve the Master for what they will benefit from Him (area-boy servants). They leave when they get what they want.
2. Those who serve Him for their leaders' sake (eye-service servants). They are only zealous when their leaders are there.
3. Those that serve Him to please their husbands, wives, parents, sponsor, congregation, children, Pastors etc. (approval-seeking servants).
4. Those that serve because they don't have any other work or source of income (contract servants). Their life span in the service of God is temporary.
5. Those who serve Him because they love and appreciate the work HE did for them on the cross see it as a privilege to be called (true servants of God). They are immovable and fervent.

Which category are you in?

Are you serving God for money, wealth, riches, healing etc.? If you receive these things, will your service in the house of God remain the same? If that Pastor, mother, father, or sponsor is moved out, will you still serve the

Lord? Let's examine ourselves. Serving the Lord in spirit and truth will bring your permanent change of story.

PRAYER: *Father, in the name of Jesus, I pray that the zeal to serve the Lord despite the happenings around us be bestowed unto us. That we will be hot for the Lord, our love for God and His kingdom will not diminish, and we will not be cast away, in Jesus' name.*

Day 73

Fear Not! You Are More Than They Are

Bible Reading: 2 Kings 6:8-22

"And he answered, Fear not: for they that be with us are more than they that be with them" **(2 Kings 6:16).**

Good morning, Family of God, the Revealer of every secret. Praise Jesus! Our God is an awesome God and dwells forever, doing wonders from generation to generation, HALLELUJAH!

He is the God of yesterday and today and will still be God tomorrow. He will never change. The servant of Prophet Elisha rose early and went forth, behold, a host compasses the city both with horse and chariots. And his servant did unto him, Alas, my master! how shall we do? **(2 Kings 6:15).**

Do you have a similar scenario? Have you woken up to see your problems staring you in the face? Are you asking the question, how shall I do? I have come with the word of God to tell you, "Fear not, for they that are with you are more than they that are with them" You are too defended to be a victim. The only challenge Christians have is blindness, a lack of knowledge of who they are and who their Father is. They have often belittled the Almighty God and His word. Knowing who you are will keep you in command of all the affairs in your life. The Bible says, "My people are destroyed for lack of knowledge **(Hosea 4:6)**. We are kings and priests unto our God **(Revelation 1:6)**. Every king has guards, and every president or Governor has guards. If this is true of the world system, how much more with God? The Bible says, "He shall give his angels charge over you.." **(Psalms 91: 11)**. They are ministering angels who have been sent to do our bidding. The knowledge of this will keep you joyful in the midst of any form of harassment. Are your challenges too many, and you cannot see your way through? Fear not! Are you afraid of being put to shame? Fear not! Is your family crisis more than you can bear? Fear not! Jesus is with you always till the end of the age.

What do you do then?

1. Pray and ask the Lord for specific needs.
2. Be confident that He has heard you.
3. Do not run away from your challenges. Go out and face them squarely. You will see that they will become nothing before you. David ran towards Goliath and conquered the giant **(1 Samuel 17:48)**. The GOD of Elisha and the God of David are still the same today!

PRAYER: *I pray that our eyes be opened to see "the horses of fire round about you" I come against every spiritual blindness. I come against ignorance. I declare that The Spirit of boldness comes upon every one of us to conquer our challenges today. Congratulations in advance, in Jesus' mighty name.*

Day 74

The Famine Is Just for a While; Stay Focused

Bible Reading: Genesis 26:1-14

"Then Isaac sowed in that land, and received in the same year an hundredfold: and the LORD blessed him " **(Genesis 26:12).**

Good morning, Family of the Overdo God, He has done exceeding abundantly above what we have asked Him. Hallelujah!

Famine in any land is not new. It has been there in times past. Abraham experienced it **(Genesis 12:10)**, Isaac experienced it **(Genesis 26:1)**, Jacob experienced it **(Genesis 42:2)**, and the kings of Israel experienced it. But what you do in the time of famine determines whether you will emerge as a wonder or be caught in its web.

What to do in the time of famine?

1. **Change direction:** Abram changed the direction of his journey and went down to Egypt **(Genesis 12:10)**. And came up out of Egypt with great riches **(Genesis 13:2)**.

2. **Sow your seed:** Isaac sowed in that land and reaped a hundredfold in the time of famine, and the Lord blessed him, and the Philistines envied him **(Genesis 26:12)**.
3. **Search for fertile land:** Jacob sought where there was grain and sent his children to go there **(Genesis 42:2)**.
4. **Decide to go forward**, like the four lepers **(2 Kings 7:4-5)**.

Complaining and murmuring will never change the famine. It will only intensify your problems. The Bible says, *"You have gone round this mountain for too long, tell my people to go forward"*. The children of Israel went forward, and the red sea parted. Jordan stood and rose upon and heap. As Jacob's sons went forward, they met with their brother Joseph, the controller of all the food they needed. As Isaac sowed, he reaped a hundredfold. As the lepers rose and went forward, God magnified their footsteps, and they became celebrities that day. God turned the situation of all Israel around because of four lepers who were cast away, rejected and stigmatized.

It doesn't matter where you are today. Dare to rise and change direction, do something new, and seek guidance through prayer. Don't do the same thing and expect a different result. Dare to step out. Your footsteps will be magnified. If you have NO for an answer, do not give up, it means Next Opportunity (NO). There is a YES (Your Expectation Satisfied) out there. The Lord of times and seasons will meet you at the point of your need.

PRAYER: *Father, in the name of Jesus, I pray for divine direction. I declare that we shall not be victims in this time of famine. I pray for hundred-fold returns and great riches to be our portion. I pray for our "Joseph" to meet with us and change our stories. We will not sit still and die; we will go forward and live in the mighty name of Jesus.*

Day 75

Your Kingdom Service is a Seed

Bible Reading: 2 Kings 8:1-6

"And when the king asked the woman, she told him. So the king appointed unto her a certain officer, saying, Restore all that was hers, and all the fruits of the field since the day that she left the land, even until now" (**2 Kings 8:6**).

Good morning, Family of the King of kings whose mercy endures forever. Praise the Lord!

The Lord sees the end from the beginning. Our times and seasons are in his hands. He makes all things beautiful in His time. The Shunammite woman returned to her hometown after the famine. The Lord had sent her away from the land. On her return, she lost all that belonged to her.

However, God ordered her feet to meet the king at the right time, and restoration came without stress. The seed she sowed in Elisha's life exempted her from all forms of suffering, famine and losses. What seed are you sowing? What are you doing for the Lord?

While the earth remains, seed time and harvest will not cease **(Genesis 8:32)**. Brethren, every good you do in this kingdom will speak for you. No service to the Lord is wasted. He is a rewarder of them that diligently seek Him **(Hebrews 11:6)**. Sow a good seed today and secure your tomorrow.

PRAYER: *I pray that all the good seeds sown in the past years, months, and weeks will speak for you today. Before you call, the Lord will answer. Your testimony will be told by many in the name of Jesus.*

Day 76

Endure to the End

Bible Reading: Romans 11:25-29

"The gifts and calling of God are without repentance" **(Romans 11:29)**.

Good morning, Family of the Faithful God. There is no turning of shadow with Him. Hallelujah! (Note: Gifts but 1 calling). Eyes have not seen, nor ears heard, nor has it come to the heart of man what God has prepared for those who love Him and are called according to His purpose **(1 Corinthians 2:9)**.

Has GOD called you? Are you in the place of your assignment? Are you forsaking all to follow him? Can you be counted worthy of His calling? Yes, a prize awaits the faithful servants at the end, but are you willing to pay the price? No price, no prize! Discover what God has called you to do and pursue it (that is ministry). Being called into a race is not a guarantee of winning the prize. You need to run this race with knowledge. Running to get a prize is running by the rules; remain on your path.

Paul commended the Thessalonians for their faith, love, endurance, and patience in serving the Lord. He said these are *"the manifest token of the righteous judgment of God, that ye might be counted worthy of the kingdom of God"* **(2 Thessalonians 1:5)**. Bearing these fruits will keep you in the race and gain you the prize at the end.

Arise, pick up the baton again, and run to the end. Don't give up on yourself, and don't be discouraged. Those that jeer at you today will cheer you at the end. Look up, and focus on the prize. Run by the rules, don'tdon't look back, don'tdon't wait, endure hardness, and finish up. Looking towards the finishing line, Jesus says to you, "well done, good and faithful servant, enter into the kingdom." Pay this price today and receive the prize tomorrow.

PRAYER: *I pray this morning that our Lord Jesus Christ will count us worthy of this calling and fulfill all good pleasure of His goodness, and the name of the Lord Jesus will be glorified in you wherever you go. I pray that those that jeer at you will be the same that will cheer you tomorrow in Jesus' name.*

Day 77

Don't be a Victim!

Bible Reading: 2 Thessalonians 2:1-5

"Let no man deceive you by any means: for that day shall not come except there come a falling away first and that man of sin be revealed, the son of perdition." (2 Thessalonians 2:3).

Good morning, Family of God, the Father of our soon-coming King. Our Lord Jesus is coming soon, Hallelujah!

Remember, the Lord's coming will be preceded by the falling away of many **(2 Thessalonians 2:3)**, the love of many waxing-cold **(Matthew 24:12)**, many being deceived out of the way, even the elect **(Matthew 24:24)**. Have you pondered on these things?

The many spoken of will be from the church, some zealous brethren, some prayer warriors, some choristers, and even some pastors. It is not by your power nor might nor by your zeal that you are standing today. It is by His grace.

Therefore, glory not in your strength and wisdom but in His strength **(Jeremiah 9:23)**. Be vigilant, be watchful, for the deceiver goes to and from the earth, looking for whom to destroy **(1 Peter 5:8)**. Be not carried away by 'strange power, signs and lying wonders' in these last days.

Who are the likely victims?

1. The miracle seekers.
2. Those who have pleasure in unrighteousness
3. Those who do not receive the love and the truth.
4. Those who believe in lies.
5. Those who are looking for healing and not the Healer, salvation and not the Saviour, miracles and not the Miracle worker.

There will be a massive release of servants of Satan in these last days with great power and signs and wonders. But the Bible says, *"hold on to the traditions which ye have been TAUGHT, either by WORD or the epistles"* **(2 Thessalonians 2:13)**. Great men of God have fallen from glory because of whom they have joined themselves with **(1 Kings 13:11-25)**. Great destinies have been destroyed because of invitations to "come and see." Let's hold fast to what we believe and wait for our Lord Jesus. He will come when he comes.

PRAYER: *I pray that our challenges will not deviate us from the truth of the word of God, that our love will not wax cold, our zeal for the things of God will not diminish, our hope will not be deferred, and our needs will be met speedily, in the mighty name of Jesus.*

Day 78

Locate Your Place in Life

Bible Reading: Genesis 2:8-15

"And the LORD God took the man and put him into the garden of Eden to dress it and to keep it" **(Genesis 2:15).**

Good morning, Family of the Wonder-Working God. He is faithful, hallelujah!

Work is a fundamental right given to man by God. Man, originally, was not created a beggar or a schemer. He was not created to depend on another man but to be connected to His maker. He was meant to "dress and keep" the garden God had planted for his benefit. What then came into man that has brought so much poverty and joblessness to him? He lost Eden. He lost his placement in Eden. But did he lose his ability to work? No! We have been redeemed and returned to Eden, the garden of God, through the Lord Jesus Christ. Why are some spirit-filled, tongue-talking Christians still on the welfare list, begging? Some use their placements in the body of Christ to force men to give as it is their right.

Paul in Thessalonians 3:7-8 said, "neither did we eat anything for naught, but wrought with labor and travail with labor, that we might not be chargeable to any of you. Paul worked and still served the Lord, David worked as a king and still prayed 5 times a day, Daniel served as one of the presidents in Babylon and still prayed 3 times a day **(Daniel 6:3,10)**, Abraham was a cattle rearer and still kept his relationship with God, **(Genesis 13:2-4)**, Isaac was a farmer and was still close to his God **(Genesis 26:2,12)**, Jacob, reared animals and still prayed to God **(Genesis 32: 9-14)**. Why are Christians ignorant? Serving God is not an escape route from work. There is dignity in work. One of the rewards of work is profit (money). Money is a defense, but a lack of it is an offense. It answers all things. It is time to stop seeking help "in the name of the Lord" and start working to be a blessing. Rise, there is a garden of Eden planted by God for you.

Seek it, and you will find it. If your certificate has been a barrier to finding that garden for years, drop it and search for it. If pride and ego are your barriers to finding that garden, drop them and search again. If ignorance is your challenge in finding it, get wisdom and search again. Your garden of Eden was created for your comfort and well-being upon the earth before He brought you to this world. Don't blame it on the devil. You have the power over him as a child of God, break that band of wickedness and find your garden. Your gold, precious stones, river, and all fruits are within your garden **(Genesis 2)**.

ARISE AND WORK!

PRAYER: *I pray this morning that you, Lord, will open our eyes to see our garden. Destroy every barrier to our work and fulfillment. Every pride and ego to getting into our garden today be broken. We will be blessed to be a blessing; we will be blessed in the field of all our endeavors, in Jesus' name.*

Day 79

Made by God

Bible Reading: Mark 1:17

"And Jesus said unto them, "Come after me and I will make you to be fishers of men" (Mark 1:17).

Good morning, Family of our Maker, who dwells in Zion. To accept the call of God is to surrender all. To become His servant is to collapse all your ambitions and plans into His will. Paul said, "It is no longer I that liveth but Christ who lives in me" **(Galatians 2:20)**. It is the one who called you that will MAKE you. Jesus said, "If any man wishes to come after me, let him deny himself and take up your cross and follow me." **(Matthew 16:24)**.

Do you still carry your old ways, friends, and thoughts in your walk with Jesus? Renew your mind. He wants to make you. The process of being made requires patience: the breaking, the pruning, the melting, the heating, and the molding are some of the processes of being made. Fishing for men needs a different skill and different instruments. You can't bring your old ideas into the new assignment given to you. He that called you has the blueprint of the new assignment He has called you into; let Him make you. The processes involved might not be palatable, but you will come out as gold to be desired by all.

What, then, do we do?

1. Acknowledge Him as your Master.
2. Surrender all to Him.
3. Enquire from Him every decision you want to take (you are now His).
4. Trust in the Lord with all your heart.
5. Seek not the praises of men.
6. Withdraw often to a solitary place to pray.
7. Be patient; wait on Him.

Your calling is not of man but God. So go on, do the bidding of your Master, men's resistance notwithstanding.

PRAYER: *Father, give us the grace to surrender all to you, let this week bring divine solutions our way, and let our caller visit us with great rewards as we serve Him, in Jesus' name.*

Day 80

Change Your Approach!

Bible Reading: Mark 2:18-22

"And no man putteth new wine into old bottles: else the new wine doth burst the bottles, and the wine is spilled, and the bottles will be marred: but new wine must be put into new bottles" **(Mark 2:22).**

Good morning, Children of the God of new beginnings. His love is new every morning. Hallelujah!

Man's problem is doing the same things and expecting a different result. Thus, we have a "busted" generation who are frustrated, downgraded, angry, and envious children even in the kingdom. Jesus began to do new things that marveled the world. He became a wonder because he changed the norm. Do you wish to make an impact and change your family history, business, environment, marriage, ministry, or relationships? Then it's time to get new bottles of the new wine. You can't be a man to be wondered at if you still do the things people are used to seeing you do. The four friends of the paralyzed man changed their approach and became a wonder to many; a teaching session became a healing service **(Mark 2:4)**. Jesus became a wonder to many because he came with a different doctrine.

Do you desire a change of story?

Then change direction and approach concerning your circumstances. Taking the same direction every day will take you to the same destination. Violent faith is the answer to your questions. Jesus said, Arise, take up your bed and go home **(Mark 2:11)**. Stretch forth your hand **(Matthew 12:13)**, little girl, arise **(Mark 5:41)**. These they obeyed, and their long-awaited answers came. If you don't get up and start moving toward your desired answers, God will not move. Start doing what you have not done before, and you will see what you have not seen. God is waiting for you.

PRAYER: *Father, in the name of Jesus, I pray that we will not die by the pool of Bethesda, we will not remain paralyzed, we will not remain lame, and we will not remain poor and hungry. Our days of change-of-story are here. Father, I pray for the power to change our direction to come upon us today. To get up and possess our possession. I declare that the spirit of the wonder-working God will possess and take us into our new beginnings, in Jesus' name.*

Day 81

The Church

Bible Reading: Mark 3:1-10

"And he entered again into the synagogue and there was a man there which had a withered hand" **(Mark 3:1).**

Good morning, Family of our merciful God. His mercy endures forever. Hallelujah!

The church is a coming together of men and women with different mind-sets and motives. The church during the life of Jesus was no different.

Which category are you in?

1. The sick (physical, spiritual, soul).

2. The accusers/ judges/gossip.

3. The true worshippers.

4. The disciples.

Are you among the accusers of men? Are you looking around for faults? Are you a self-employed judge in the house of the Lord, or are you a disciple of Jesus? A house divided against itself cannot stand. A kingdom divided against itself cannot also stand. Let's search ourselves are we truly working for the Master or working for the accuser of the brethren?

God has not called us as judges in the church but to heal the sick, preach the gospel, open the prison doors to them that are bound, cast out demons (not work with and for them), love unconditionally, be there for the brethren even when they are rejected, strengthen the feeble knees, stand in the gap for our brethren deceived by the devil. The devil has been the most subtle being from the beginning. Be watchful, be vigilant for the devil your adversary is seeking for whom to destroy **(1 Peter 5:8)**.

Let's examine our actions and thoughts, the actions you have taken, are there for or against the progress of the body of Christ, the progress of the children of God or are they dividing the house of God? Accusing spirits, judgmental spirits, the spirit of disobedience, gossip, envy, hatred, strife, variance, and wrath are all instruments of the devil used to divide the church. Go not near these, touch not these unclean things. The instruments that build the body of Christs: are love, joy, peace, long-suffering, gentleness, goodness, faith, meekness, and temperance **(Galatians 5:22)**. Take hold of these things. Be a builder and not a divider.

PRAYER: *Father, in the name of Jesus, I pray this morning that the devil will not use us against the kingdom of God, the evil-spirit of the accuser of the brethren is cast out of our midst, I pray that we will be called the disciples of Jesus in all ramifications. We come against every spirit of sickness, physically, mentally, and spiritually in the body of Christ, in the mighty name of Jesus Christ.*

Day 82

Speak to Your Storm!

Bible Reading: Mark 4:35-40

"Why are ye so fearful? How is it that ye have no faith? " **(Mark 4:40).**

Good morning, Family of the Good Shepherd. He wakeneth us morning by morning and causes us to hear as the "learned." Hallelujah!

What is the state of faithlessness? It is a state of having the Word of God with and in you and still panicking in the face of trouble. Many Christians have panicked and asked the same question to the Master of the universe, who is also their Master and Lord, saying, *"Carest thou not that we perish?"*

Jesus, the Word of God, was in the boat with them. When challenges came, they forgot all the words he had spoken to them. They forgot all the miracles he had done afore time. They forget that they have power inside of them.

Have you noticed the different stages involved in processing the word of God? Some hear the word of God, and IMMEDIATELY, the devil steals the word. Some hear the word and IMMEDIATELY receive it but forget when faced with challenges. Some hear the word, get too busy to process it, and lose it. Some hear the word, receive it, and bear fruits 30, 60, or 100 folds.

Your level of faith depends on the level of the word received in your spirit. Faith comes by hearing and hearing the word of God **(Romans 10:17)**. Are you fearful? Go for the word. Are you asking questions you have the answers inside of you? Are you facing storms after a prophecy has gone ahead of you? Jesus said, "let's go over to the other side." But they arose a storm afterward. That storm is not to kill you and cannot stop you from reaching your destination. Why?

1. Jesus is in that boat with you.
2. You have the power inside of you.
3. He cannot send his word without fulfilling what had been sent.
4. Jesus is in you and can be called up immediately.

Why, then, are you so fearful? Stand up, rebuke that wind, and the raging sea will be calm. "Why criest thou to me," God said to Moses, "speak unto the children of Israel that they go forward" (Exodus 14:15). I have come with these words also for you, "Stand up, wipe those tears, speak to the storms and go forward." The Master of the storms is in that boat.

PRAYER: *I pray today that the Lord will activate the word that has been sleeping inside us and boost our confidence. We rebuke by faith the raging storm and speak peace to every troubled home, marriage, ministry, business, and mind. To the nation Nigeria, we speak peace in the name of Jesus.*

Day 83

Wipe Your Tears

Bible Reading: Mark 5:35-42

"And when He was come in, He said unto them, why make ye this ado, and weep, the damsel is not dead but sleepeth" (Mark 5:39).

Good morning, Family of the Resurrection and the Life. He is alive forevermore, hallelujah!

Certain cases have been closed by men. Certain burials took place because men were ignorant of what was to be done to revive the dead. Likewise, certain businesses, marriages, ministries, and doors were shut down, not by the Lord but by men.

Have you wept over your situation because you have concluded it and named it an impossible case? Are you counting age and time? Are you saying, I am in my 40s or 50s, I can't marry again, I can't have that child again, I can't go to school again, I can't be employed again, I can't have that appointment anymore, I can't reach that goal anymore, how can I answer the call of God in my 50s or 60s? Where will I get the money to buy that car, house, or marriage? It is an impossible case; this is my fate.

"Why weepeth thou, that damsel is not dead but sleeping," Jesus said. The Resurrection and life are here, the God of all possibilities is here, the Master of the universe is here, the owner of times and seasons is here, the God of Abraham at 75 years is here, the God of Sarah at 90 is here, the God that made Sarah still attractive at 65 years is here, the God that raised Lazarus and Jairus daughter from the dead is here, the Lord that brought Joseph out from prison and gave him a national job, "executive car" to tour Egypt, a wife, and a palace in one day is here, the God that turned Mordecai, the gatekeeper to a Vice president in one day is here...

This list is inexhaustible. Are you still in doubt? Why are you laughing like Sarah did, Is anything too hard for the Lord? This word is for you, yes, you. It is not just a devotional but is sent specifically to you. That situation is not a closed case. To anyone who cares to believe, there shall be a performance of these things which are told you from the Lord **(Luke 1:45).**

PRAYER: *I declare this morning by the word of the Lord, "TALITHA CUMI" ARISE, COME ALIVE!" I speak to every closed case, be revived now, businesses, marriages, children, ministries, whatever case was closed by the devil, we speak life unto them. Let the spirit that raised Jesus from the dead raise all those closed cases again. Let the bone find its bone. Let things begin to fix themselves up. Let praises and shouts of joy begin again in every home that dares to believe in the mighty name of Jesus.*

Day 84

Toil No More

Bible Reading: Mark 6:48-52

"And he saw them toiling in rowing, for the wind was contrary unto them ... and he saith unto them be of good cheer, it is I, be not afraid" **(Mark 6:48, 50)**.

Good morning, Family of the Almighty God. Our God does wonders, Hallelujah!

Toiling is working extremely hard or incessantly to labor, struggle, sweat, and plow away. Does that sound like what you have been doing; sweat, plow away? Adam sinned in the garden of Eden, and a curse was pronounced upon him. God said unto *"Adam, ... in sweat thou shall eat bread, till you return to the ground"* **(Genesis 3:19)**. But there is good news for every child of God; sweating and toiling had been erased from our Kingdom. Jesus came and paid the price for us. He became a curse and saved us eternally from its consequence. Blotting out the handwriting of ordinances against us which was contrary to us and took it out of the way, nailing it to His cross **(Colossians 2:14)**, Hallelujah!

But why are we still toiling as Christians?

1. Lack of knowledge of what Christianity is (Christianity is not going to church and being a busybody).
2. Having Jesus around you but not having Him in your boat.
3. Having no wisdom and understanding of the workings of God.
4. Being guided by the workings of this world, which are controlled by the 5 senses.
5. Not working by faith (Seeing into the supernatural and working in the natural to bring the things seen in the supernatural to the natural world).

The days of ignorance are over. Jesus is walking on your troubled sea. Get wisdom and get Him into your boat to end your years of toiling. Have you been working on your own? Have you been toiling all along while having Jesus all around you? Do you see Him as a Principal partner in whatever you are doing? Talk with Him in every step of your dealings, not only kneeling to "pray," for some do the ritual of "praying" but not talking with the Lord. They forget what they ask as soon as they stop praying. Deliberately lay your challenges and plans before the Master. This morning He says to you," Be of good cheer, it is I, be not afraid."

PRAYER: *Father, in the name of Jesus, I pray that the grace to bring Jesus into our boat be given to us. I pray that every toiling, sweating, struggling, and laboring as children of the Most-High God ceases this moment. I ask that wisdom and understanding of the workings in the Kingdom be bestowed unto us, in Jesus' mighty name.*

Day 85

You Are Your Thoughts

Bible Reading: Mark 7:15

"There is nothing from without a man that entering into him can defile him, but the things which come out of him, those are they that defile the man" **(Mark 7:15).**

Good morning, Family of The Good Shepherd. Great is His name, hallelujah!

Brethren, this is our week of the harvest of testimonies. But testimonies are born out of tests. Are we tested on all sides, are we tempted by the devil in our thoughts? Are we ready to overcome and pass the numerous trials and temptations that will bring victories our way? Out of the abundance of the heart, the mouth speaks **(Matthew 12:34)**.

The state of our heart determines the words we speak. The Bible says, "Guard your heart with all diligence for out of it comes the issues of life" **(Proverbs 4:23)**. The issues of our lives are products of the thoughts in our hearts. In your heart are either good or evil thoughts. Evil thoughts defile a man, but good thoughts bless and elevate a man. For as a man thinks in his heart, so is he **(Proverbs 23:7)**. You are not higher than your thoughts.

A fornicator became a fornicator in his heart first, before he performed the act; a liar thought in his heart before he lied, every evil proceeds from the heart before it is acted on the outside. Likewise, a kind, humble, peaceful, joyous, gentle, or victorious person is one in the heart before it is performed on the outside. Faith and fear are of the heart. The action determines what is on the inside.

The Lord sends His word to us saying, "Guard your heart with all diligence, for out of it are the issues of life". The outcome and happenings around you are mostly determined by you; you either reject it or watch it. Do you see all things as possible because you have the Almighty God as your Father, or do you think of impossibilities and place boundaries on what He can or cannot do?

How healthy is your heart is determined by:

1. What you read and meditate on (Psalms 1:2).
2. What you constantly see or watch (Joshua 1:8).
3. What you constantly hear (Romans 10:17).

These can either corrupt or enhance your heart. Philippians 4:8 says, "Finally, brethren, whatever things are true, whatever things are honest, whatever things are just, whatever things are pure, whatever things are lovely, whatever things are of good report, if there is any virtue and if there is any praise think on these things."

You have the power to stop any unholy and defiling thought. You are the programmer of your thought pattern. Arise and erase all evil thoughts by reprogramming your heart with the word of God. As a man thinks in his heart, so is he because what is abundant in your heart, your mouth will begin to speak and create them.

PRAYER: *I pray that the grace to reprogram our thoughts will be given unto us. I pray that the mind of Christ in us will be activated. I cast out every strategy of the enemy to use our minds against us. Our faith to move mountains will be given to us this morning, in the name of Jesus.*

Day 86

The Way Maker Is On Duty

Bible Reading: Mark 8:1-9

"And his disciples answered him, from whence can man satisfy these men with bread here in the wilderness? And He asked them, "How many loaves have ye?" (Mark 8:4-5).

Good morning, Family of the Great Provider. The God of the Children of Israel in the wilderness is worthy of praise. Hallelujah!

Have you asked this question, or are you wondering how God will meet your needs in this dwindling economy? How will you solve the problems facing you right now? I come with this good news "HE IS ABLE."

The God that furnished a table in the wilderness, providing manna and meat for millions, has not changed. He came again and gave seven loaves of bread to 4,000 men in the wilderness. He is the same yesterday, today, and forever. Stop looking at the economy. Stop looking back at how much your salary or income has been. The God that rained down manna from heaven is your God. The God that gave 4,000 men bread from seven loaves of bread is still working here on the earth. You might be asking, how shall this be? The power of the Holy Spirit will accomplish it. What do you have now in your hand?

1. Lift it up
2. Give thanks to the Father
3. Break it
4. Begin to use it.

The miracle-working God, the multiplier God, is at work. You will not run dry, the cruise of oil, the little in your hand will not diminish until your heart's desire materializes. Rise, do not doubt, pick that little you have and follow your Father.

PRAYER: *Father, in the name of Jesus, I pray that you will activate the mustard seed faith in us, and the spirit of understanding will come upon us. I cast out every doubt and fear. I destroy every near-success syndrome in anyone's life today. Father, breathe upon us the breadth of life; every dead or dying part of our life comes alive right now, in the name of Jesus.*

Day 87

You Are the Salt of the Earth

Bible Reading: Mark 9:49-50

"Salt is good, but if salt has lost its saltiness where with shall it be seasoned" **(Mark 9:50).**

Good morning, Family of God. Our God is good all the time. Hallelujah!

What is salt used for? It is used as a preservative, a seasoning, it is used to give taste to food, and it strengthens the bones. The bible says, we are the salt of the earth **(Matthew 5:13),** not of the church. Do you discover your purpose on the earth and the reason for your rebirth? Yes, we are born again so we can make heaven. But why are we still here after giving our lives to Christ?

If a purpose of a thing is not known abuse is inevitable. We are called to make the world a better place, we are called to preserve humanity, to add sweetness to the world around us, to strengthen the feeble knees. We are not the salt of the church but of the earth. Are you only a Christian within the confines of the church but make no meaning to lives outside the church? Jesus went about doing good and healing all that were oppressed of the devil **(Acts 10:38)**; that is a true Salt. Joseph put smiles on faces wherever he went; in Potiphar's house **(Genesis 39:5)**, in the prison **(Genesis 40:7)**, in the palace **(Genesis 41:37)**, among his family members **(Genesis 45:10-11)**; that was a true salt.

Are you an active salt of the earth or have you lost your saltiness? Why have you stopped blessing lives? The bible says, "Be not weary on well doing for in due season we shall reap, IF WE FAINT NOT" **(Galatians 6:9, emphasis mine)**. Men cannot reward you, the one that called you is your Rewarder. Men have paid you back evil for your good, but that has not changed the truth that you are the salt of the earth.

Your value and what God had placed inside of you is not a function of man's opinion. In due season the Rewarder will come and will make you a pillar in this kingdom. The light affliction you are experiencing now cannot be compared to the weight of glory ahead. Do not lose your saltiness, do not lose your relevance on the earth on the basis of criticism. Pick up where you lost it, begin to add value, give hope to the hopeless, serve the Lord with gladness, strengthen the feeble knees, encourage the downcast and the heart broken. Freely ye have received freely ye give **(Matthew 10:8)**.

The spirit of the Lord had been poured upon every child of God to continue with the work that Jesus did **(Luke 4:14)**, preach the gospel to the poor, heal the broken hearted, preach deliverance to the captives, recover sight to the blind, set at liberty the bruised. This is how to be true salt of the earth. Job was salt in his days; eye to the blind, feet to the lame, father to the poor... Job 29:15, His Rewarder came in due season for him **(Job 42:10)**.

PRAYER: *Father in the name of Jesus; I pray that where we lost our saltiness that our Father that can do all things will restore it.*

Day 88

Unforgiveness

Bible Reading: Mark 11:25-26

"And when ye stand praying, forgive, if any aught against any, that your father which is in heaven may forgive you your trespasses" **(Mark 11:25).**

Good morning, Family of the ever-loving Father. Great are you, Lord!

What is forgiveness? It is the intentional and voluntary process by which a victim changes feelings and attitude regarding an offense, lets go of negative emotions such as vengefulness, and forswears recompense for or punishment of the offender. Has anyone wronged you knowingly or unknowingly? Have you kept these offenses in your heart? Have you covered it under the carpet, or have you pretended to forgive, but deep down in your heart, you still have the hurt, pain, and revenge? Brethren, you are hurting yourselves, not anyone, the offender, God but yourself.

What Are the Dangers of Unforgiveness?

1. You stand unforgiven no matter who you are **(Mark 11:26)**.
2. Your prayers cannot receive answered prayers **(Mark 11:24-25, Isaiah 59:1)**.
3. You open the doors for Satan to lord over your affairs **(Matthew 9)**.
4. Your heavens remain closed.
5. Your faith cannot move any mountain **(Hebrew 11:6)**.
6. God cannot accept your offering **(Matthew 5:23)**.
7. You are separated from your father. That puts your life in danger and opens you up to Satanic attacks **(Isaiah 59:1-2)**.

Wives, husbands, Ministers, sons, daughters, parents, brethren, brothers, sisters, mothers, and fathers have blocked their heavens through unforgiveness. Examine yourself again; are you living in unforgiveness? No one is worth making you miss heaven and all the blessings God has kept for you here on earth.

Go and settle it, FORGIVE, let go of your husband, wife, colleague, brother, sister, mother, father, Pastor, member, neighbor, friend... Your blessings, healing, deliverance, peace at home, business, ministry progress, and open heavens link to that forgiveness. Settle with those involved. Free your heart, and your hanging blessings will begin to drop. You are the architect of your life. GOD has sent those blessings, heart desires, children, etc., to you, but there is no landing place. FORGIVE now, yes now. God has sent this word for your upliftment. Swallow your pride and FORGIVE.

PRAYER: *Father, in the name of Jesus, let your Spirit come upon us to enable us to forgive as you do, to cleanse our hearts of every trace of hurt against any. I pray for the heavens to open unto us and let down each of our hanging blessings. Dear Lord, let testimonies spring forth this morning in the name of Jesus.*

Day 89

You Are an Ambassador

Bible Reading: 2 Corinthians 5:15-20

"Therefore, if any man be in Christ, he is a new creature, old things are passed away behold all things are become new" **(2 Corinthians 5:17).**

Good morning, Family of the Creator of the universe. Great is our God, Hallelujah.

Christ died and redeemed us from destruction, adopted us into His family, justified us, and appointed us as Ambassadors of Christ under the Ministry of reconciliation. Brethren, have you been looking down on yourself? Have men despised you? Do you have low self-esteem and do not know your place in the kingdom? For My people are destroyed for lack of knowledge **(Hosea 4:6)**. A man that is in honor and understandeth it not, is like the beast that perisheth **(Psalms 49:20)**. A son that does not know his rights and inheritance in His father's land, will fall victim of wicked men in the land.

Do you not know that you have been paid for, adopted into the Highest Kingdom: Kingdom of the Most-High God? You have been cleansed, sanctified, justified, and made an ambassador in the kingdom? Every ambassador has responsibilities, and yours is to reconcile men to God.

Ambassadors are immune to punishments in the land of their assignment. They have their medical bills, food, and comfortable shelter paid for in the currency of their land of origin. In essence, they have rights and privileges that they enjoy.

What are the privileges of an Ambassador of Christ? (Exodus 23:25-27)

1. The kingdom of God provides for your needs.
2. The Lord blesses your food.
3. A sickness-free life.
4. Fulfilled number of days.
5. Nothing is permitted to be barren in and around you.
6. The Lord preserves your children.
7. You become a terror to your enemies.
8. The Lord drives your enemies from your land.
9. You are to eat the good of the land **(Isaiah 1:19)**.
10. You are to spend your days in prosperity and your years in pleasure **(Job 36:11)**.

The devil has blinded the minds of God's people, so they do not see and claim the rights that accrue unto them in redemption. Brethren, resist the devil, and he will flee from you. You can't spend your energy fighting and never entering Canaan all your life. Whatever has a beginning has an end; there is an end to every wickedness. Arise and possess your possession. The doors to your healing, deliverance, breakthroughs, peace, joy, riches, and increase are still open. No man or powers can shut it **(Revelation 3:8)**.

Though they are many adversaries to delay, distract, and blind you, they do not possess the ability to deny you of your possession. Arise and possess your possession; you can't be fighting forever **(Psalms 46:9)**. There is a time of rest for God's people; declare the year of Jubilee. The land of Israel had rest from war for 40 years **(Judges 3:11)**. Know who you are in Christ; you are an Ambassador for Christ, decked with power from on High, to reconcile men to God.

If you have served the Master in any area in the kingdom, you are entitled to accrued benefits, the devil notwithstanding **(Psalms 23:5)**. Welcome to your year of Jubilee, your year of rewards. Welcome to your season of remembrance. I see you smiling and rejoicing. I see you held by Jesus into your place of honor. I see him taking you to your throne.

PRAYER: *Father, thank you for making us Ambassadors in the kingdom. Release your angels to ward off every delay, sickness, bareness, lack, want, and whatever has been planted by the devil. We pray for the release of our accrued blessings. When men are saying there is a casting down, raise us. As darkness covers the people, let your light shine on us. We declare that the old things pass away and all things become new, in Jesus' name.*

Day 90

It's Your Time

Bible Reading: Isaiah 40:1-5

"Every valley shall be exalted, and every mountain and hill shall be made low: and the crooked shall be made straight, and the rough places plain:" **(2 Corinthians 5:17).**

Good morning, Family of the Omnipotent God. He is too faithful to fail.

Brethren, Our God is a God of times and seasons. He appoints a time for every purpose on the earth **(Ecclesiastics 3:1)**. To the children of Israel, their time of deliverance was 400 years **(Genesis 15:13-14)**. To Daniel and his people, it was 70 years **(Daniel 9:2)**. Joseph's time of redemption came. God sent His word, loosed him, and let him go free **(Psalm 105:19)**. The time of John came. He was shown forth to Israel **(Luke 1:80)**. The time of Sarah to have Isaac came, and God sent his word in her direction. She brought forth her Isaac **(Genesis 21:1)**.

God sets a time for every man's lifting, promotions, deliverance, release, laughter, end of wars, and favor **(Psalms 102:13)**. When it is your time and season, things begin to fit into their proper places. Struggles, failures, sorrow, pain, neglect, abandonment, exercise in futility, labor without profit, seeking without finding, crying with no answers all cease. God begins to position men in strategic places to favor you.

Brethren fear not; that vision is for an appointed time. As the sun rises in the skies and the moon disappears without struggles, so shall your time come without struggles. The good news is, it's your time of favor **(Psalms 102:13)**. Cry no more! His word is sent to someone this new month, saying, *"Comfort ye, comfort ye my people, saith your God. Speak ye comfortably to Jerusalem, and cry unto her, that her warfare is accomplished, that her iniquity is pardoned: for she hath received of the Lord's hand double for all her sins. The voice of him that crieth in the wilderness, prepare ye the way of the Lord, make straight in the desert a highway for our God. Every valley shall be exalted, and every mountain and hill shall be made low: and the crooked shall be made straight, and the rough places plain: And the glory of the Lord shall be revealed, and all flesh shall see it together: for the mouth of the Lord hath spoken it."*

It's your season. It's your time. Arise, take up your journey, and cross over your Jordan (meaning, flowing down or one who descends). Enough is enough of your going down, flowing down, and descending. It's time for your rising. Congratulations, your time has come!

PRAYER: *Father, thank you for bringing us into our season of rising. We pray that you straighten every crookedness, level every perpetual hill, scatter every everlasting mountain, and let our glory come alive, in Jesus' name.*

Day 91

It's Time to Move

Bible Reading: Acts 12:5-10

"And the angel said unto him, Gird thyself, and bind on thy sandals. And so he did. And he saith unto him, Cast thy garment about thee, and follow me "(Acts 12:8).

Good morning, Family of the Good Shepherd, He is too committed; He cannot abandon us halfway, hallelujah.

Brethren, He who began a good work in us can complete it. Many times, ignorance of the word of God and lack of understanding of the happenings around our lives and the seasons we are can rob us of our inheritance in God. Many spend days, weeks, months, and even years crying and asking God for what He has released since the 1st day they asked for it. They fail to lay hold of understanding of the workings of God. They fail to understand the place of wisdom and faith in drawing down their blessings and working in the reality of the answered prayers.

Peter was kept in prison awaiting execution by Herod, but the church prayed for His release. God sent his angel as they prayed to answer their prayers. Peter also must have prayed in prison for God to rescue him. His answers would have been futility if he was not sensitive in the spirit to hear the angel's voice as he instructed him. His answer would have been far-fetched if he had been overwhelmed by the challenge. His answer would not have come to reality if he did not obey the instructions to get up and move. God told the Israelites, *"I have sent my angels to go before you to lead you in all your ways."*

If you do not move, they will not move. The angels are sent to go before (in front) you. You determine if that door opens on its own accord, you determine if the angel will open that closed door or not. A sensor door opens when you move towards the door. No amount of prayer will open that door if you do not go towards it.

We sometimes want God to do everything for us, spoon-feed us, open the door, and come back and carry us through it; that is irresponsibility. For any miracle to be affected, we have our part to play. We need to move. God told the children of Israel to go forward. His part was to part the sea. The angel was to open the prison doors, but Peter had to get up and walk towards the door. Jesus told the man with the withered hand to stretch forth his hands. His part was to heal him.

We are the carriers of the miracles we are looking for; we carry the keys to that open door we are crying for; we determine whether the angel sent to us will open the doors to our breakthrough. What is your disposition when the angel arrives to lead you out of your challenges and take you to your desired place? Do your challenges blind you that you cannot see the angel nor hear the one sent to rescue you? God is not a wicked God, never! When you call, He answers, and when you knock, He opens. But are you ready to get up, put on your shoes, and follow him out? God had sent His word. The angel had been waiting for you to arise and work towards the door of your prison.

Get up, stop the tears, stop the murmuring, stop the prayers for now, and begin to do something. Begin to get your things to move out of your predicament. You have moved around this mountain for too long. Get up and go forward. Everything will move when you move. God wants to see your faith; faith is an action word, and there is no faith without works. Get up and get your angel moving. He is looking back to see whether you are following him. Where you stop is where he will stop. When you move, he will lead you.

Get up; now is your time! The good news is, your prison door will open of its own accord as you move towards it. What you cried for will come like a dream in the night, and you will be set free.

PRAYER: *Father, thank you for your word. Give us the grace and the strength to get up and follow the angel you have sent to rescue us. Help us not to wallow in our tears anymore. Please help us to showcase your loving kindness, tender mercies, and faithfulness to the world. Help us to be sensitive in the spirit to hear when you instruct us, in Jesus' name.*

Day 92

Destined for Glory

Bible Reading: Genesis 31:1-9

"And your father hath deceived me, and changed my wages ten times; but God suffered him not to hurt me" **(Genesis 31:7).**

Good morning, Family of the Omniscient God, He sees the end from the beginning, praise Master Jesus!

Brethren, sometimes life throws at you what you do not expect. So is the path of great men. Many get battered and beaten, rejected, and deceived. Ups and downs, mountain and valley experiences, feelings of giving up, and throwing in the towel all characterize great men's lives. Their journey to the top is usually challenging and trouble-free. Jacob, the covenant child of Isaac, whom God said concerning him, "Esau I hated but Jacob I loved" **(Romans 9:12)**. He did not have it easy to become the father of the 12 tribes of Israel (a nation chosen by God). More than that, he became the father of the 12 tribes of Israel whose names formed the 12 gates in heaven **(Revelation 21:12)**. What glory!!!

However, the journey to that glory was not without troubles, rejections, mistakes, battering, and beatings. Jacob became a servant to his Uncle, who changed his wages ten times. He left his father Isaac's riches and ran to a place where he was humiliated **(Genesis 31)**. Joseph, a name that has gained so much glory today for preserving Israel from decadence, did not gain this glory on a platter of gold, but through suffering, rejections, and imprisonment, he reached his destined glory **(Genesis 37)**.

Moses, a known "prince" in Egypt, was rejected by his relatives and declared wanted by Pharaoh. A prince became a Shepherd in Midian. Those 40 years tending the sheep, beaten by rain, scourged by the sun, hit by hunger and thirst in the bush while feeding the sheep. However, he still gained glory at the end **(Exodus 2-3)**.

Jesus, the King of kings and the Lord of lords, was included on this pathway to glory. He was betrayed, rejected, beaten, battered, neglected, and denied. The same men he fed and healed did not forget his kindness. They preferred the thief to their Healer and Saviour, but these did not take his destined glory from Him. Today, He is the King of kings and the Lord of lords **(Luke 23)**.

Are you battered, beaten, rejected, troubled, denied, or betrayed? Has life changed your wages '10 times' when you have toiled and felt that it's time for your wages and you get nothing in return for your labor? Don't be dismayed, give up, or be discouraged.

Congratulations to you, for you, have entered the path of greatness. No great man made it to the place of glory without passing these streets. It is worth noting that what God had destined you to be, nothing can change it. No devil can change it.

No circumstance can thwart the plan of God for your life. They can only delay, but God works everything together for your good to give you a future and hope and bring you to an expected end **(Jeremiah 29:11)**. So, cease all your worries and discouragement.

You are not alone. Your situation is not worst as others went through theirs and came out victorious. Yours will not be different. Hold on; change is coming, don't give up now. God can do what He said He would do and will fulfill everything promised, don't give up on God, for He will never give up on you. Know this, YOU ARE DESTINED FOR GLORY, AND YOU WILL DOUBTLESS GET THERE!!!

PRAYER: *Father, thank you for your word. Empower us to hold on, open our eyes to see the glory ahead of us, strengthen us in our wilderness, and take us to our place of honor and glory, in Jesus' name.*

STAY ENCOURAGED!

Join This Family of God

The word written on the pages of this book will only work effectively for those who belong to the family of God. The encouragement sent from heaven, is to believers in the finished work of Christ Jesus on the cross of Calvary.

Jesus, our Saviour, stands at the door of your heart and knocks, only those who open their heart to him will give in the power to become the sons of God. This qualifies you to be born again and become a member of the family of God.

If you want to receive the Lord Jesus Christ as Lord and personal Saviour and become a member of God's family, pray this prayer sincerely from your heart:

Lord Jesus, come into my heart, be my Lord and my Saviour, I acknowledge that I am a sinner, I believe that you came and died on the cross for the remission of my sins. I believe you rose again on the third day and now sits on the right hand of God. Wash me with your blood, forgive all my sins and make me your child. Thank you Jesus for saving me. I AM NOW YOUR CHILD!

Welcome to the Family of God!